REVISED PRINTING

Introduction to
HUMAN GEOGRAPHY
A World-Systems Approach

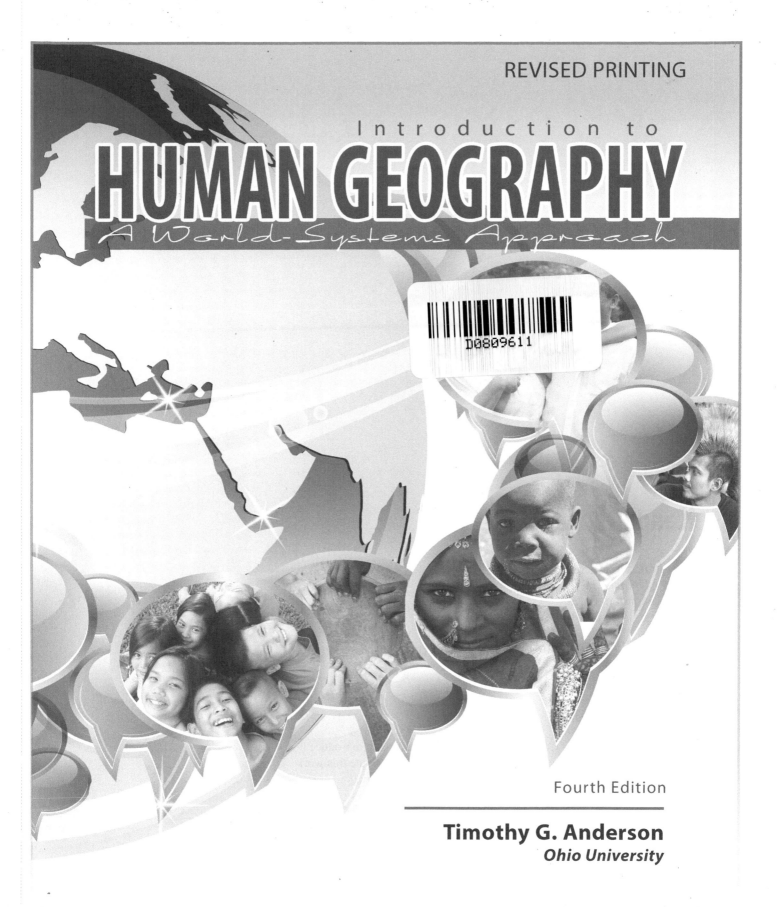

Fourth Edition

Timothy G. Anderson
Ohio University

Kendall Hunt
publishing company

Cover image © Shutterstock, Inc.

www.kendallhunt.com
Send all inquiries to:
4050 Westmark Drive
Dubuque, IA 52004-1840

CONTENTS

CHAPTER THREE

CHAPTER FOUR

CHAPTER FIVE

CHAPTER SIX

ACKNOWLEDGMENTS

Many individuals provided support and guidance of immense value in the writing and materialization of this text. First, I would like to thank the Ohio University College of Arts and Sciences for the awarding of a faculty fellowship leave, which allowed time off from teaching duties to write the initial edition of the text. A large debt of gratitude is also due each of my colleagues in the Department of Geography at Ohio University for their support over the years. Special thanks are extended to Professors Brad Jokisch, Geoff Buckley, and Jim Dyer, colleagues and friends whose intellectual dialogue and advice, as well as collegial support, is so much appreciated. At Kendall-Hunt in Dubuque, special thanks go to Ashley Bluml, Acquisitions Editor; Abby Davis, Project Coordinator; and Beth Klipping, Author Account Manager. All three were professional, courteous, and patient throughout all stages of the development and writing of this revised fourth edition, and they offered helpful advice on many occasions. I also thank the hundreds of students at Ohio University who have taken Geography 1200—Human Geography—with me over the past 15 years. Their intellectual curiosity and desire to learn more about the world in which they live, as well as their valuable feedback about course content and the way in which it is presented, have been of invaluable assistance in the clarification and formulation of the ideas in this text. Finally, I thank my family for all of their support and encouragement during the writing of the text.

CHAPTER 1

INTRODUCTION: MAIN IDEAS AND THEMATIC STRUCTURE

In This Chapter:

THE NATURE OF GEOGRAPHY

Most Americans relate the term *geography* to the rote memorization of trivial facts associated with various countries of the world: capitals, imports and exports, highest mountains, largest lakes, most populous cities, climates, and the like. This trivialized impression of the subject matter geography covers most likely stems from the fact that, until recently, most U.S. elementary schools and high schools did not teach geography as a distinctive subject.. Even today, it is often taught as a marginalized part of social science courses in elementary schools and civics or history courses in high schools. As a result, most Americans think of geography as a collection of trivial factoids rather than as a distinct academic subject such as history, economics, mathematics, or physics. But, within academia, geography is a thriving, diverse discipline with its own set of theories, research methods, terminology, and subject matter, and it has a unique way of looking at the world. Indeed, the Association of American Geographers, the largest professional society of geographers in the world, counts over 5,000 professors, students, and professionals as members.

So what do geographers do? What is their method of analysis? What questions do geographers ask about the world? These questions, as it turns out, are not easily answered. Indeed, any two geographers might answer them in very different ways, for geography is not unified by subject, but rather by method. This is yet another reason for the public's misconceptions about what geography is and, indeed, for misconceptions many academicians themselves have. Geography does not seem to fit into academe the same way that other subjects do because the discipline is not unified or defined by its subject matter. Rather, it is unified and defined by its method and approach, its mode of analysis. This mode of analysis (or approach or perspective) involves a **spatial perspective**. In this way, geography can be conceptualized as a way of thinking about the world, space, and places. This spatial (geographical) perspective involves the fundamental question about how both cultural and natural phenomena vary spatially (geographically) across the earth's surface. As such, it is possible to study the geography of almost any phenomenon that occurs on the earth's surface. Employing these ideas, we may define the academic discipline of geography as *the study of the spatial variation of phenomena across the earth's surface.* So, geographers do not study a certain thing, or subject. Instead, they study all sorts of things and subjects in a specific way—spatially.

The eighteeth-century German philosopher Immanuel Kant understood very well the unique position that geography held within academia. Kant argued that human beings make sense of and organize the world in one of three ways, and human knowledge, as well as academic departments in the modern university, is arranged or organized in the same way. First, Kant wrote, we make sense of the world *topically* by organizing knowledge according to specific subject matter: biology as the study of plant and animal life, geology as the study of the physical structure of the earth, sociology as the study of human society, and so on. Each of these fields is unified by its subject matter. Second, according to Kant, we make sense of the world *temporally* by organizing phenomena according to time, in periods and eras. This is the sole domain of the discipline of history. Finally, Kant argued that we make sense of the world *chorologically* (geographically) by organizing phenomena according to how they vary across space and from place to place. This is the sole domain of the discipline of geography. The disciplines of history and geography are similar in that they are both unified by a method rather than the study of a specific subject matter. The region (discussed below) in geography is analogous to the era or period in history—they are the main units of analysis in each of the respective disciplines.

Figure 1.1 represents a generalized model for understanding the nature of the academic discipline of geography. This figure illustrates the field's three main subfields: physical geography, human geography, and environmental geography. The description and analysis of patterns on the landscape unites each of these subfields. When most people think of the term *landscape,* they think of something depicted in a painting, or perhaps a garden. But, when geographers employ the term landscape, they are referring to the totality of our surroundings. In this sense, the **physical landscape** refers to the patterns created on the earth's surface by natural or physical processes. For example, tectonic forces create continents and mountain chains; Long-term climatic processes create varying vegetative realms; Wind and water shape and modify landforms. **Physical geography**, then, is the subfield of geography that is concerned with the description and analysis of the physical landscape and the processes that create and modify that landscape. The various subfields of physical geography, such as biogeography, climatology and geomorphology, are natural sciences, allied with such fields as botany, meteorology and geology, and, like these allied fields, research in physical geography is undertaken largely according to the scientific method.

Human geography is the subfield of geography that involves the description and analysis of cultural landscapes and the social and cultural processes that create and modify those landscapes. While physical geography concerns the natural forces that shape the earth's physical landscapes, human geography analyzes the social and cultural forces that create cultural landscapes. The **cultural landscape,** then, may be conceptualized as the human *imprint* on the physical landscape resulting from modification of the physical landscape by human social and cultural forces. Given the power and influence of human technology and institutions, many human geographers see human beings as the ultimate modifiers of the physical landscape. The various subfields of human geography, such as historical geography, economic geography, and political geography are social sciences, allied with such fields as history, economics, and political science. In addition to their own research methodologies, human geographers often employ research methods from these allied fields. Traditionally, human geography has pertained to how

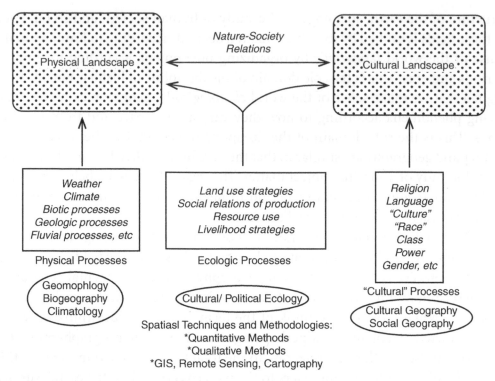

Figure 1.1 The Geographic World-View

cultural processes such as religion, language, and worldview affect the cultural landscape. More recently, however, cultural geographers have begun to question traditional ideas about how cultural landscapes are created by focusing on so-called post-structural processes to reevaluate the nature of cultural landscapes. In such research, the cultural landscape is conceptualized as a stage upon which social struggles dealing with such concepts as race, class, power, and gender are played out. In this sense, the cultural landscape is the product of such struggles.

Although not all geographers recognize it as such, it can be argued that **environmental geography** is a third major subfield of geography. Environmental geography involves the interrelationships between humans and the natural environments in which they live, or nature-society relationships. Environmental geographers study the patterns created on the landscape by such interactions and the processes involved, such as social relations of production, cultural adaptations or maladaptations to particular environments, modifications to the environment wrought by human economies and technologies, and the use (or misuse) of natural resources.

UNIFYING THEMES IN GEOGRAPHY

The discussion in the previous section illustrates the diverse nature of the academic discipline of geography. In spite of this diversity, however, we can identify some common themes most geographical studies address, which unify the field. Three common concepts have already been identified: pattern, process, and landscape. In addition, we can delineate five unifying themes in geographic research:

Location

This theme addresses the question, "where is it located?" We can think of location in two primary ways. **Absolute location** refers to a specific point on the globe—latitude and longitude, for example. On the other hand, **relative location** refers to the location of a place or phenomenon with respect to other places or phenomena around it. For example, some places may occupy a more central role regarding the economy of a country. Such places may be said to occupy a more central relative location.

Place and Space

This theme refers to the description and analysis of the patterning of phenomena in a certain place or across space. This patterning can be analyzed in terms of the distribution, density, and concentration of phenomena.

Human-Environment Interaction

This theme explores the complex relationships between human beings and their natural environment, how people interact with the environment around them, the nature of that interaction, and the influence of the natural environment on human culture. Interpretations of the role the environment plays in human affairs and the nature of human-environment interaction have changed substantially over time. The ancient Greeks, for example, attributed observed cultural differences around the world to the climates in which people lived. It was argued that African cultures differed from European cultures because African societies evolved in a hot climate. That is, they argued that the environment plays a deciding role in terms of shaping cultural values, ideals, and traditions—certain environments and climates create certain cultures. This supposition is known as **environmental determinism**. Surprisingly, social scientists continued to use this argument to account for cultural differences around the world well into the twentieth century. Some prominent American geographers in the early twentieth century, for example, argued that a unique subculture punctuated by poverty, subsistence agriculture, and a distinctive folk culture (food, music, social systems, etc.) developed in Appalachia because of the region's mountainous terrain and geographical remoteness. But, under close scrutiny, of course, environmental determinism is an untenable supposition that does not explain reality. Culture is not created by the climate of a place or by mountains—culture is learned behavior passed on from generation to generation.

By the 1940s, the use of environmental deterministic arguments to explain culture began to wither under close scientific scrutiny. Led by French human geographers beginning in the 1930s, the idea of **possibilism** began to replace determinism. This supposition argued that the environment surrounding us offers certain possibilities, but what people do with those possibilities is determined by cultural values and traditions that are learned and that evolve over time. Today, geographers have modified possibilism into a workable hypothesis that may be termed **environmental perception**. This hypothesis argues that different cultures perceive or conceptualize the environment in which they live in different ways. These differences in perception may be attributed to differences in cultural values and traditions, which result in the creation of varying cultural landscapes. In this way, it is argued, any cultural landscape can be "read," analyzed, and deconstructed to understand the values, ideals, and traditions (the culture) of the people who created that landscape.

Movement

This theme seeks to understand how and why observed phenomena move through space—"how did this pattern or distribution come to be?" The central concept geographers employ to explain the movement of people, ideas, and innovations from place to place is **diffusion**. In this sense, cultural diffusion may be thought of as the movement of ideas, traditions, and innovations through space. Three different kinds of movement can be employed to explain how diffusion takes place. *Hierarchical diffusion* describes the movement of ideas and innovations in stair-step fashion from person to person: one person tells two people, and they tell two people, and they tell two people, and so on. This kind of diffusion is relatively slow, and it may take weeks, months, or years for ideas to move from one place to another. Before the advent of mass communication technology in the early twentieth century, most diffusion was hierarchical in nature.

A second type of diffusion is *contagious diffusion*. Contagious diffusion refers to the rapid movement of innovations and ideas through space in the same manner that a contagious disease spreads through a population. Many people (perhaps in the millions) become aware of an idea or innovation at the same time. In today's age of globalization, the internet, and highly evolved methods of mass communication, contagious diffusion is the primary way in which ideas move from place to place.

A third type of diffusion is known as *relocation diffusion*. Relocation diffusion describes the movement of ideas over long distances in a relatively short time, usually attributed to mass migrations of people from one place to another place. The fact that the majority of North Americans speak English as a mother tongue and practice some form of Christianity can most likely be attributed to the migration of millions of Europeans to North America over some 400 years (relocation diffusion) and the subsequent movement across the continent (contagious diffusion).

Regions

The **region** is the primary unit of analysis for the geographer. A region is a bounded area of space within which there is homogeneity of a certain phenomenon or phenomena. Historically, the region is a central concept in geography that is employed to delimit and define spatial differentiation. Both physical and human geographers use the concept of region to describe and analyze places and subject matter. In this sense, a **culture region** is a place within which a certain culture is predominant. It should be noted, however, that ways in which regions are defined might differ from person to person; all types of regions are the product of human reasoning and as such are often cultural and socially constructed.

The geographers Robert Ostergren and Mathias Le Bossé identify three primary types of regions. **Instituted regions** are created by authorities within some kind of organization (such as governments and businesses) primarily for administrative purposes, such as planning, or for collecting data or revenue. The boundaries of such regions are usually clearly demarcated and agreed upon by almost everyone. In many cases, instituted regions consist of nested hierarchies of subregions. An example of this idea would be the nested hierarchy of federal, state, and local political boundaries in the United States and other federal states. **Denoted regions** are usually created by academics to reduce the complexity of the real world using systems of classification. Places in a denoted region are grouped together because they share one or more commonalities. Like all regions, they are the product of the person or persons who create them, and as such, their boundaries are often open to debate and critique.

Denoted regions can be subdivided into two different subtypes. **Formal denoted regions** are those that are rather easily identified using verifiable data. **Functional denoted regions** are areas in which the places in the region are all tied to a common central place by the movement of people, ideas, and things. A good example of a functional region is a trade area or the market area of a good or service. A **Perceptual region** is a region created informally, without official sanction by people within a community, or perhaps by those outside of a community. The boundaries of such regions are often imagined or internally perceived in the minds of the inhabitants based on real or perceived commonalities (such as language, religion, or ethnicity). By their very nature, perceptual regions are socially constructed, and therefore, subject to debate and continuous reinterpretation.

WORLD-SYSTEMS ANALYSIS

The main goals of this text are to give students a basic understanding of the world's human geography, delineate the world's major culture regions, illustrate how human culture and cultural landscapes vary across space, and examine the phenomenon of economic *development* and *underdevelopment*. To accomplish these goals effectively, we will employ the concepts of pattern, process, and landscape, as well as the five themes outlined above. In addition, **world-systems analysis** is used as a thematic context around which the book is structured. World-systems analysis is best described as a distinctive approach to the study of social change developed by the American sociologist Immanuel Wallerstein in the early 1970s. This approach combines economic, political, sociological, geographical, and historical aspects in a holistic, historical social science that is based on three different research traditions: dependency theory, the French *Annales* School of history (especially the work of Fernand Braudel), and Marxist theory.

World-systems analysis chiefly involves analysis of the nature, development, and structure of the capitalist world economy and provides a useful context within which to compare and contrast regions of relative development and underdevelopment in the world's economy through time and space. In his four-volume work *The Modern World-System*, Wallerstein maintains that there have been only three fundamental ways, or **modes of production**, in which societies throughout history have been organized to sustain production. These modes of production, these societies, can be distinguished by determining the division of labor in production that is dominant in these societies.

The *reciprocal-lineage mode of production* refers to a society in which production is differentiated mainly by age and gender, and exchange is merely reciprocal in nature (that is, barter exchange dominates the economy). Wallerstein calls such systems *mini-systems*, and there have been countless numbers of these throughout history. Such societies are usually small in terms of population and geographical area, and there are few, if any, class divisions (anthropologists refer to such societies as *tribes*).

The *redistributive-tributary mode of production* describes a class-based society in which a large agricultural underclass that pays tribute to a small ruling class performs production; anthropologists refer to such societies as *chiefdoms*. Wallerstein calls these societies *world-empires*, and there have been many of them since the Neolithic Revolution around 10,000 B.C.E. (examples would include the ancient kingdoms of Mesopotamia and the Nile Valley, the Mayan and Aztec societies in Middle America, various kingdoms in western and southeastern Africa, the ancient dynasties of China, and the Ottoman and Roman empires). World-empires were very large in terms of population and geographical size.

Finally, the *capitalist mode of production* also refers to a class-based society, but is distinguished by the goal of a ceaseless accumulation of capital operating within a market logic and structure (capitalism). Wallerstein calls such societies *world-economies*. According to Wallerstein, there has been only one successful world-economy. It originated in Western Europe around the middle of the fifteenth century and spread to encompass the entire world by the beginning of the twentieth century through long-distance sea trade, colonialism, and world conflicts. World-empires and world-economies are called *world-systems* by Wallerstein because the divisions of labor operating within them are larger than any one local grouping.

In world-systems analysis, then, the world is seen as a single entity—a capitalist world-economy. Wallerstein argues that to meaningfully understand the nature of the global economy and of social change, one must not consider the role of individual countries so much as the entire world-system. To do so is to commit the fundamental *error of developmentalism*, which dominates current liberal studies of development and Marxist analyses, both of which see individual countries progressing through stages of development.

DEVELOPMENT AND UNDERDEVELOPMENT IN THE WORLD-ECONOMY

One of the most useful aspects of world-systems analysis with respect to understanding the human geography of the world and its division into developed and underdeveloped realms is its delimitation of the spatial, political, and economic structure of the current capitalist world-economy. According to Wallerstein, the capitalist world-economy that has developed since the mid-fifteenth century has three primary structural features:

1. A single world market that operates within the context of a capitalist ideology and logic; this logic and ideology affects economic decisions throughout the entire world-system.

2. A multiple-state system in which no single state (country) dominates totally and within which political and economic competition among various states is structured and defined.

3. A three-tiered economic and spatial structure of stratification in terms of the degree of economic development and underdevelopment of the world's various states. This textbook employs this basic three-tiered structure as the primary tool, as a model and a theory, for understanding basic differences in the human geography of the world today and in the past. In place of terms like "developed world" and "developing world," or "first world" and "third world," we will use the terms *core, semi-periphery,* and *periphery,* which are employed in world-systems analysis to differentiate between regions of varying economic development in the world. This text argues that an understanding of the differences between these regions is fundamental to a meaningful appreciation of the differences in such things as the nature of cultures, the structure of economies, political organization and population issues, and problems around the world.

Table 1.1 below employs widely available socio-economic statistics for selected countries to illustrate general socio-economic differences between core, semi-peripheral, and peripheral regions. While the terms *core* and *periphery* are employed to indicate geographical location in common usage, in world-systems analysis, they do not *necessarily* refer to a state's geographical location on

TABLE 1.1 World Demographic/Socio-Economic Indicator Data, 2014

COUNTRY	POP	BR	DR	NI	IM	TFR	<15	>65	GNI/PPP
World	7,238	20	8	1.2	38	2.5	26	8	$14,210
More Dev.	1,249	11	10	0.1	5	1.6	16	17	$37,470
Less Dev.	5,989	22	7	1.4	42	2.6	29	6	$8,930
Least Dev.	916	33	9	2.4	64	4.3	40	4	$1,220
Selected Core States									
Germany	80.9	8	11	−0.2	3.3	1.4	13	21	$44,540
Japan	127.1	8	10	−0.2	1.9	1.4	13	26	$37,630
USA	317.7	13	8	0.4	5.4	1.9	19	14	$53,960
Norway	5.1	12	8	0.4	2.5	1.8	18	16	$66,520
Spain	46.5	9	8	0.1	3.1	1.3	15	18	$31,850
Selected Semiperipheral States									
Russia	143.7	13	13	0.0	10.3	1.7	16	13	$23,200
South Africa	53.7	20	11	1.0	42	2.3	29	5	$12,240
Costa Rica	4.8	15	4	1.1	8.7	1.8	24	7	$13,570
Argentina	42.7	19	7	1.1	11.7	2.3	25	10	$14,090
Mexico	119.7	19	6	1.4	13	2.2	28	6	$16,110
China	1,364.1	12	7	0.5	15	1.5	16	10	$11,850
Malaysia	30.1	17	5	1.3	7	2.1	26	6	$22,460
Saudi Arabia	30.8	22	4	1.8	16	2.9	30	3	$53,780
Selected Peripheral States									
Pakistan	194.0	28	8	2.0	74	3.8	38	4	$4,920
Laos	6.8	26	6	2.0	68	3.2	35	4	$4,570
Bolivia	10.3	26	7	1.9	42	3.2	35	5	$5,750
Dem. Rep. Congo	71.2	46	16	3.0	109	6.6	46	3	$680
Nigeria	177.5	39	13	2.5	69	5.6	44	3	$5,600
Malawi	16.8	40	12	2.9	66	5.5	45	3	$760

POP = Population (millions)
BR = Births/1000 persons/year
DR = Deaths/1000 persons/year
NI = Natural Increase/annum (%)
IM = Infant Mortality Rate (deaths of infants under 1 per 1,000 live births)
TFR = Total Fertility Rate (average number of children born to a woman during her lifetime)
<15 = Percentage of population less than 15 years of age
>65 = Percentage of population greater than 65 years of age
GNI/PPP = Gross national income in purchasing power parity/population (US $) (2013)

Source: Population Reference Bureau, 2014 World Population Data Sheet http://www.prb.org

the globe. Rather, they are used to refer to a state or region's "location" in the world-economy, that is, on the "inside" (core), on the "outside" (periphery), or somewhere in the middle (semi-periphery) of the world-economy in terms of relative control. Those states in the core control and direct the world-economy, while those in the periphery are most often controlled and directed by the core states. Further, history shows us that it is clear that core and periphery are not geographically or temporally static—states move up and down within this hierarchy over time at a non-constant rate. A recent excellent example of this rule is the former Soviet Union. Before its breakup in late 1991, one could argue (using socio-economic data) that the Soviet Union was a core state. Since the breakup, however, economic conditions have deteriorated to the point that Russia is now clearly a semi-peripheral state. Further examples would include several countries in Southeast Asia, such as Indonesia, Thailand, Malaysia, and Singapore. Peripheral states until the 1980s, they all are now part of the semi-periphery due to surging manufacturing economies and greater political and economic stability.

Core States

The **core states** of the world-economy today include most states in northern, western, and southern Europe; the United States and Canada; Japan; and Australia and New Zealand. It is from here that the world-economy is directed and where its primary command and control centers, such as New York, London, Paris, Frankfurt, and Tokyo, are located. Western Europe emerged as the first core region of the capitalist world-economy in the mid-fifteenth century and remained the primary core until the twentieth century, when the United States, Canada, Japan, and Australia and New Zealand joined its ranks. The wealth of the core stemmed at first from highly efficient agricultural production and control of merchant capitalism through long-distance sea trade in valuable tropical agricultural products (such as tea, coffee, sugar, tobacco, cotton, and spices) during the era of colonialism. Portugal, Spain, the Netherlands, and the United Kingdom were the successive **hegemonic powers** (dominance in economic, political, military, and cultural world affairs) of this early world-economy from the mid-fifteenth century until the early twentieth century.

The United States emerged as the primary hegemonic power after World War II. From this period until the early 1970s, the wealth of the core was based primarily on dominance in industrial capitalism focused on heavy industry (cars, ships, chemicals, manufacturing, and the like). The United States, Canada, the Soviet Union, Germany, and Japan all emerged as the major players in world industrial production during this era. With the exception of the Soviet Union, all of these states remain in the core today. Since the early 1970s, post-industrial restructuring in the core economies has taken place, with a switch away from a reliance on heavy industry to a focus on service industries and information technologies. This era is generally called the era of *globalization,* which is characterized by a pronounced international division of labor (this will be discussed further in Chapter 2).

In comparison with semi-peripheral and peripheral locations, the core states all have highly developed economies that are oriented toward service industries and post-industrial technologies, such as information technology and computer software production. These advanced economies enjoy a very high standard of living, high gross national products, and per capita incomes, and are generally the "richest" countries in the world. Other characteristics of the core states include stable, democratic governments with large militaries; low infant mortality rates and high life expectancies (measures of relative health and availability of adequate health care); low birth rates, fertility rates, and rates of natural increase (all signs of very low population growth rates); and large urban (as opposed to rural) populations.

Peripheral States

The **peripheral states** of the world-economy today are located primarily in Sub-Saharan Africa, South Asia (Pakistan, India, and Bangladesh), and parts of Southeast Asia (e.g., Papua New Guinea, Cambodia, Laos) and some parts of Middle and South America (e.g., Guatemala, Bolivia, Haiti). The peripheral states all have several things in common. Historically, they are all former colonies of core states and, accordingly, are generally located in either subtropical or tropical areas. During the era of merchant capitalism and colonialism, these areas were assigned a specific role in the world-economy by the dominant core powers: to be producers of valuable tropical agricultural goods such as sugar, tea, coffee, cotton, and spices. As colonies, these areas lost political sovereignty to colonial governance by the core powers, and traditional economies and societies were replaced by a colonial economy focusing on plantation agriculture linked heavily with the core. The core powers employed slavery and peonage as the primary form of labor control in the periphery. Most of these former colonies regained political sovereignty after the end of the colonial era, beginning in the late nineteenth century, but have struggled since then to rebuild economies and societies that were heavily disrupted by colonialism.

Today, the economies of the periphery remain largely agricultural. The majority of the populations in these countries rely on subsistence farming, low-wage labor on agricultural plantations, or low-skilled, low-wage service positions in urban areas. Compared with the core and the semi-periphery, living standards are relatively low, as are per-capita incomes—these areas are among the "poorest" countries in the world. Peripheral regions are plagued by myriad problems today: weak, inefficient, and often corrupt governments; political instability; ethnic conflict; weakly developed economies and a lack of public services (such as regular electric service, availability of clean water, and public sewage services) taken for granted in core regions;. High infant mortality rates and relatively low life expectancies belie weakly developed health-care systems and a susceptibility to epidemics and chronic problems with diseases such as malaria and AIDS. While core states have very low rates of natural increase (or even negative population growth in some countries), the peripheral populations are the world's fastest growing populations. Compared with the core and semi-periphery, the peripheral states have very high birth and fertility rates and "young" populations—a significant proportion of these populations is younger than fifteen years of age. If core populations can be described as "old" with stable growth rates, then peripheral populations can be characterized as "young" and growing rapidly.

Semi-Peripheral States

The **semi-peripheral states** today include many of the countries of Middle and South America (e.g., Mexico, Costa Rica, Chile, Brazil, and Argentina), Eastern and Southeastern Europe (e.g., Russia, Poland, Bulgaria, and Hungary), Southwest Asia (e.g., Turkey, Saudi Arabia, and Iran), and Southeast and East Asia (e.g., Indonesia, Malaysia, Thailand, China, and South Korea). Other semi-peripheral outliers include such countries as South Africa and much of Saharan Africa (e.g., Tunisia, Algeria, and Libya). As the term implies, the semi-periphery occupies a middle place in the hierarchy of development in the world-economy. If one considers socio-economic indicators and demographic data, it is clear that the data for semi-peripheral countries are midway between the extremes of the core and periphery—per capita incomes, birth and fertility rates, and rates of natural increase in the semi-periphery are neither the highest nor the lowest in the world, but rather fall somewhere in between. Accordingly, many world-systems analysts characterize semi-peripheral countries as not the richest, but certainly not the poorest countries in the world.

Many, but not all, of these countries are also former colonies. But, since the 1960s, most of them have managed to achieve some amount of economic and political stability, largely with loans from the World Bank and foreign aid from the core countries. As a result, however, many are saddled with large debts to the World Bank and banks in the core. Economic stability in these countries was largely achieved through a focus on heavy industry and manufacturing as central features of the economy under the authority of rather strong (and sometimes corrupt and heavy-handed) central governments. At the same time, most semi-peripheral economies still depend heavily on the agricultural sector. Indeed, one of the most characteristic aspects of the semi-periphery is a mixed economy dependent upon agriculture (largely for export to the core), heavy industry and manufacturing, and a small but growing service sector. Social stratification in semi-peripheral societies reflects this mixed economy: a large rural agricultural lower class; a relatively large, urban blue-collar manufacturing class; and a small, wealthy urban professional class.

This intense social stratification—a vast difference between the richest and poorest members of society—is one of the hallmarks of the semi-periphery. According to Wallerstein, the most pronounced and acute class struggle occurs in the semi-periphery. This class struggle is often accompanied by chronic political and economic instability. The semi-periphery is also the focus of periodic restructurings of the world-economy during times of economic stagnation, which provide the necessary conditions for this restructuring. For example, the semi-periphery usually is most adversely affected by crises in the world-economy. During the Industrial Revolution in the late eighteenth and early nineteenth centuries, for example, traditional agricultural and artisan economies in places such as Germany and Ireland (part of the semi-periphery at that time) were upset by the changes wrought by industrialism in Great Britain. Many farmers and artisans who could no longer make a living at home moved to core regions like Great Britain and the United States to take jobs in urban factories, thus supplying the core with a needed industrial workforce. In today's world-economy, a similar situation is occurring in the semi-periphery. This time around, traditional economies are being reordered by the current restructuring usually called globalization. This restructuring involves the outsourcing of manufacturing jobs by multi-national firms from the core to the semi-periphery, especially in the textile industry (the manufacturing of clothes, shoes, and the like). At the same time, this economic reordering has again resulted in traditional economies being upset and phased out. One of the consequences of this has been a renewed large-scale migration of low-skilled farmers and laborers from the semi-periphery (Latin America, East and Southeast Asia, Southwest Asia) to the core (Western Europe, North America, Australia).

This restructuring has resulted in a pronounced **international division of labor** characterized by economic specialization in each of the three regions of the world-economy. Peripheral economies are dominated by subsistence agriculture, plantation agriculture, and natural resource extraction, all mainly for export to the semi-periphery and core. While local, low-wage labor is employed in the production of these resources and products, the capital and management is often controlled from or by the core in the form of multi-national corporations. Semi-peripheral economies specialize in small-scale commercial agriculture, heavy industry and manufacturing (steel, chemicals, etc.), and textile production, the latter for export primarily to the core. Core economies are highly diversified but are primarily service-based. That is, most workers are employed in the service sector of the economy, which includes everything from retain sales to real estate, banking, health care, education, government, and high-tech industries such as computer software production. Commercial agriculture is an important part of the economy in all of the core countries, but relatively few people make a living wholly as farmers (typically less than 10 percent of the population). While heavy industry and manufacturing was the mainstay of the industrial economies of the core from World War II until the 1970s, employment in this sector of the economy and its overall importance to the economies of the core have declined dramatically over the past 20 years.

Summary

This chapter has discussed the nature of the discipline of geography, outlining its main themes, its place in academia, and its distinctive way of looking at the world around us. It has also introduced some of the main themes with which this text is concerned and outlined its primary goals, namely general patterns in the human geography of the world, with an emphasis on the following:

- A basic understanding of the major culture regions of the world, where these regions are located, their general characteristics, and their attendant cultural landscapes

- An appreciation of how populations vary from place to place around the world, what populations "look" like, how they are structured, and various problems and policies related to population in different parts of the world
- A comprehension of the various ways in which people make a living around the world, how economies and societies are structured in different parts of the world, and the nature of the world-economy today and in the past
- An understanding of the concepts of economic development and underdevelopment, and how critically important these are in understanding the nature of economies, societies, and ways of life around the world both today and in the past

This chapter has also introduced the basic premises of world-systems analysis and presented it as a general model for understanding the development of capitalism in the world-economy and for comprehending its nature and structure today. The three-tiered spatial and economic hierarchy of core, semi-periphery, and periphery will be used as a thematic context and as a model, within which various regions of the world might be placed. It is argued throughout the text that virtually all aspects of differences in the human geography of the world, especially with respect to the goals outlined above, can be more fully understood within the context of this world-systems model. As is the case with any model, it must be understood that this model simplifies reality to a certain extent. The model is useful in understanding *general* global patterns and differences, especially at the regional level. It is hoped that through the application of this model, students will gain a fuller comprehension of the myriad ways in which the human geography of the world varies from place to place and from region to region.

KEY TERMS TO KNOW

Spatial Perspective

Physical Landscape

Physical Geography

Human Geography

Cultural Landscape

Environmental Geography

Absolute Location

Relative Location

Environmental
  Determinism

Possibilism

Environmental Perception

Diffusion

Region

Culture Region

Instituted Region

Denoted Region

Formal Denoted Region

Functional Denoted
  Region

Perceptual Region

World-Systems Analysis

Modes of Production

Mini-Systems

World-Empires

World-Economy

Error of
  Developmentalism

Core States

Hegemonic Powers

Peripheral States

Semi-Peripheral States

International Division of
  Labor

STUDY QUESTIONS

1. With what themes is the academic discipline of geography concerned? What are the five unifying themes of geography? In what important ways does geography differ from most other academic disciplines in terms of its subject matter and method of analysis?

_____

_____

_____

_____

_____

_____

_____

_____

2. Discuss the concept of landscape and its importance in the discipline of geography.

_____

_____

_____

_____

_____

_____

_____

3. What are the fundamental features of world-systems analysis? Discuss the basic structure of the world-economy using the terms *core, semi-periphery,* and *periphery.* How does world-systems theory conceptualize and explain economic "development" and "underdevelopment"?

_____

_____

_____

_____

_____

_____

_____

_____

FURTHER READING

Christopher Chase-Dunn and Thomas D. Hall, eds., *Rise and Demise: Comparing World-Systems* (Boulder: Westview Press, 1997).

Saul Cohen, *Geopolitics of the World System* (Lanham: Rowman & Littlefield, 2003).

Harm De Blij, *The Power of Place: Geography, Destiny, and Globalization's Rough Landscape* (Oxford: Oxford University Press, 2009).

James S. Duncan, Nuala C. Johnson, and Richard H. Schein, eds., *A Companion to Cultural Geography* (Oxford: Blackwell, 2004).

Derek Gregory et al, eds., *The Dictionary of Human Geography* (Oxford: Blackwell, 2009).

Thomas D. Hall, ed., *A World-Systems Reader* (Lanham: Rowman & Littlefield, 2000).

Geoffrey J. Martin, *All Possible Worlds: A History of Geographical Ideas* (New York: Oxford University Press, 2005).

Donald Mitchell, *Cultural Geography: A Critical Introduction* (Oxford: Blackwell, 2000).

Robert Ostergren and Mathias Le Bossé, *The Europeans: A Geography of People, Culture and Environment* (London: The Guilford Press, 2011).

Peter Taylor, *Political Geography: World-Economy, Nation-State and Locality* (Essex: Longman, 1993).

Immanuel Wallerstein, *World-Systems Analysis: An Introduction* (Durham: Duke University Press, 2004).

WEB SITES

Population Reference Bureau (**http://www.prb.org**).

United Nations (**http://data.un.org**).

The World Bank (**http://data.worldbank.org**).

FOUR REVOLUTIONS: THE EVOLUTION AND DYNAMICS OF GLOBAL CORE-PERIPHERY RELATIONSHIPS

In This Chapter:

Since the goal of this text is to aid the student in understanding the basic characteristics of the human geography of the world today, especially with respect to development and underdevelopment and global core-periphery relationships, then it is altogether appropriate that we understand the evolution of these relationships over time. We must start at the beginning; we must know from where we have come before we can know where we are today. What are the historical processes that have resulted in present global geographical patterns? Toward these ends, this chapter introduces general, long-term, global-scale trends in the development of the world-economy.

The chapter argues that four significant "revolutions" in human history have occurred that have successively shaped and reordered the world's economies, political geographies, cultures, and landscapes. Each revolution represents a clear break with what had come before concerning dominant modes of production, forms of labor control, social relations of production, dominant technologies in use, and the types of natural resources exploited. Each revolution resulted in a significant increase in the amount of power that could be harnessed per person per year. Further, each revolution resulted in substantial changes in the ways in which human beings conceived of the world around them, how humans perceived of themselves in the world and their place in it, and how certain natural resources could be used and exploited. Over time, the effects of these revolutions resulted in the alteration of the world's cultural landscapes into what they are today. The cultural landscapes of today reveal these past changes. They reveal changing cultural traditions, ideals, and values. They reveal social, political, and economic struggles that have taken place over time and space. The world's cultural landscapes are, in short, a palimpsest of the last 12,000 years of human history.

THE NEOLITHIC REVOLUTION

What Was It?

The first revolution to significantly alter the ways in which human beings viewed and used the natural world around them was what anthropologists refer to as the **Neolithic Revolution**. This term refers to the period in human history about 10,000–12,000 B.C.E. when the first large-scale urban settlements began to appear, together with concomitant changes in the structure and nature of societies, modes of production, and social relations of production. The most important feature of the Neolithic Revolution, however, and what engendered most of these changes, was the domestication of plants and animals. **Plant and animal domestication** refers to the gradual genetic change of plants and animals through selective breeding, such that they become dependent upon human intervention for their reproduction. Certain plants and animals, or certain varieties of plants and animals, were selected for particular qualities, such as taste or caloric value or nutritional value, while other varieties were left behind. These selected varieties of plants and animals were nurtured, protected, and cared for in gardens and fields, and they continuously reproduced. Over many generations, this caused genetic change, resulting in plants and animals with distinctive characteristics found to be helpful to human beings (again, characteristics such as taste or resistance to pests and drought). Today, this process occurs in the form of scientific genetic breeding of plants and animals carried out at laboratories and universities.

Without a doubt, the most important and far-reaching result of plant and animal domestication was the advent of agriculture on a scale that had not been seen previously. Before the advent of large-scale agriculture, the vast majority of societies all over the world could be described, in world-systems analysis language, as mini-systems, with social relations of production and social and political organizations that were tribal in nature. Exchange in these mini-systems was basically reciprocal, social classes were weakly developed, and their geographic

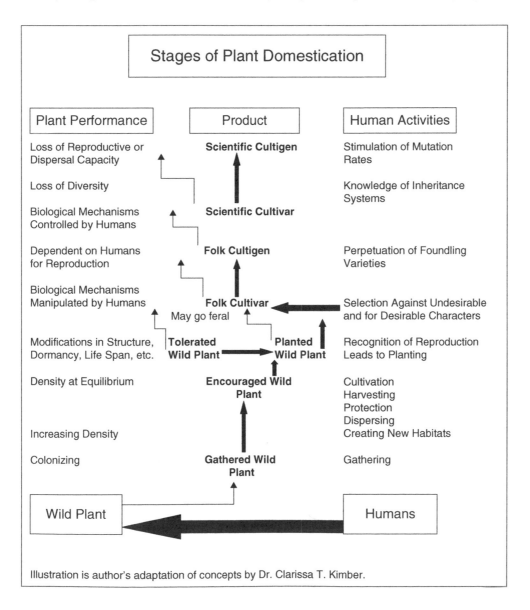

Illustration is author's adaptation of concepts by Dr. Clarissa T. Kimber.

extent was very small, amounting to little more than a claimed homeland or hunting territory. Agriculture, however, wrought social and economic changes that changed the world forever. Where it occurred, much more complex societies quickly developed, with highly stratified societies, vast increases in food production, and despotic forms of political organization that claimed and defended large territories by force. That is, where plant and animal domestication first occurred, where agriculture first originated, mini-systems gave way to the development of world-empires.

Why and Where Did It Occur?

Two primary theories exist about when, where, and why agriculture first originated. The first, what we might call the orthodox theory of domestication, is agreed upon by most historians and anthropologists. The second was proposed by the geographer Carl O. Sauer in the mid-twentieth century. The orthodox theory, that which is most widely accepted by social scientists and for which there is the most archaeological evidence, argues that plant and animal domestication occurred independently in several areas of the world at about the same time in history—from about 8,000 to 12,000 B.C.E.—through a process of **independent invention**. That is, populations in different parts of the world "invented" agriculture on their own without contact from outside populations, without learning it from others. Most experts argue that some sort of ecological stress—overpopulation or climate change, for example—forced these populations to move from a nomadic hunting and gathering type of lifestyle to a more sedentary lifestyle more and more dependent upon agriculture to feed burgeoning populations.

This revolutionary change did not happen overnight, or even in a few generations, but rather most likely occurred over hundreds of years and over many human generations. But, where it did occur, in the following so-called **culture hearths** of innovation and invention, societies began to look very different, the hallmark of which was the first urban civilizations. Table 2.1 lists some of the earliest culture hearths and gives dates by which world-empire types of civilizations had developed. The dates for the domestication of various plants and animals are not given here, but radiocarbon dating of plant and animal remains suggests that plant domestication occurred as early as 12,000 to 15,000 years ago in Southwest Asia and the Nile Valley and 5,000 years ago in Middle America and the Andean Highlands of South America.

Another less widely accepted theory of the development of agriculture was proposed by the American geographer Carl O. Sauer in his book *Agricultural Origins and Dispersals* in 1952. Sauer suggested that agricultural first developed in Southeast Asia as early as 20,000 years ago and from there diffused to the other areas of the world. This theory, therefore, is one based on the idea of **cultural diffusion** from an original hearth area to all other regions of the world. Sauer reasoned that agriculture would have developed first in an area where the richest

TABLE 2.1 Major Culture Hearths

CULTURE HEARTH	LOCATION	DATE	DOMESTICATES
Mesopotamia	Southwest Asia	by 5,500 B.C.E.	wheat, barley, rye, grapes, oats, cattle, horse, dogs, sheep
East Africa	Nile Valley	by 3,300 B.C.E.	barley, coffee, cotton, millet, wheat
Incan	Andean Highlands	by 2,500 B.C.E.	potato, tomato, llama, guinea pig, alpaca
Mediterranean	Crete, Greece	by 2,500 B.C.E.	barley, grapes, goats olives, dates, garlic
Indus Valley	Pakistan	by 2,300 B.C.E.	wheat, cattle, dog, rye, sheep, horse
North China	Huang He Valley	by 2,200 B.C.E.	soybeans, buckwheat, cabbage, barley, plum
Southeast Asia	Vietnam, Cambodia, Thailand	by 1,500 B.C.E.	bananas, chicken, pig, tea, dog, rice, taro, water buffalo, yams
Meso-America	Mexico, Guatemala	by 1,250 B.C.E.	maize, beans, taro, chili peppers, dog
West Africa	Ghana, Mali	by 400 B.C.E.	arrowroot, millets, pig, rice, oil palm,

array of different kinds of useful plants naturally occurred, most likely a tropical region, and in a place where people were not under any kind of ecological stress. Such populations, Sauer argued, would not have been *forced* to invent agriculture, but rather would have had ample time over many generations to experiment with growing different varieties of useful plants. This theory, however, is at most a thought experiment, and little archaeological evidence supports it. It also presupposes that populations in certain parts of the world were not "advanced" enough to invent agriculture on their own and that they therefore must have been shown how by invading populations having such knowledge. For these reasons, Sauer's theory is not widely held to be true.

What Changes Did It Engender?

An agricultural lifestyle had the effect of radically altering the nature and structure of societies and economies in each of the various culture hearths. Aside from new innovations and techniques that increased crop yields and food production, such as crop rotation and large-scale irrigation projects, the most revolutionary change was the development of highly stratified, agriculturally based societies with codified class structures, a class-based division of labor, and a redistributive-tributary mode of production. Anthropologists refer to such societies as *chiefdoms*, and in essence, this describes a *feudal* social and economic order. In the world-systems perspective, Wallerstein refers to these societies as *world-empires*.

At one end of the socio-economic spectrum in these societies, an agricultural underclass comprised up to 90 percent of the population. This peasant underclass produced agricultural surpluses, the storage and redistribution of which was controlled and directed by an aristocratic (title by blood birth) royalty at the other extreme of the socio-economic spectrum. These rulers also directed the building of vast agricultural projects, such as irrigation schemes (in North China and the Nile Valley), and the construction of monumental structures (such as the Great Wall and the pyramids). Such rulers (known as kings, emperors, pharaohs, and the like) are often called **god-kings** by anthropologists because they often claimed to possess supernatural powers and to have achieved communion with the gods. These rulers surrounded themselves with other elite classes, such as scribes and priests. These ruling elite lived in a central urban location known as a city-state, the basic political unit of world-empires. The presence of distinctive elite classes points to the development of other revolutionary changes first witnessed in each of these culture hearth that set the stage for the development of vastly more complex societies and economies that forever changed the ways in which humans interacted with the natural world around them:

- Written languages to keep records of agricultural surpluses and the redistribution of surpluses
- The development and use of calendars to track the seasons and to predict planting and harvesting times
- The development of an organized military under the command of the ruling elite to defend a claimed political territory
- Significant population increases as a result of more stable food supplies

THE MERCHANT CAPITALIST "REVOLUTION"

What Was It?

Although it is not always called a "revolution," the development of merchant capitalism in northwestern Europe in the mid-fifteenth century and its diffusion around the world over the ensuing 400 years engendered changes in societies, economies, and cultures that shaped the modern world-economy more than any other event. If we define **capitalism** as the production and exchange of goods and services for private money profit, then most historians would agree that it has existed for millennia in many places around the world. **Merchant capitalism**, however, arose in only one region of the world at a specific point in history—Holland and England in the mid-fifteenth century. Merchant capitalism was an altogether new version of capitalist production and exchange because it was based heavily on long-distance sea trade in exotic products from the tropics and subtropics.

Because such products were rare and costly to acquire (it took five years to travel by ship from Holland to the southeast Asian spice islands in the sixteenth century), the high relative value of such trade meant great wealth to the countries and individuals that controlled it. Before the advent of merchant capitalism, most trade was merely regional in nature and used land-based caravans or shipping routes that plied coastal regions. Merchant capitalism involved the use of new sailing and navigation technologies to strike out into the oceans out of sight of land on risky overseas ventures in search of rare tropical goods for which Europeans were willing to pay high prices (such as sugar, cotton, tea, coffee, pepper, and other spices). In short, merchant capitalism ushered in the era of colonialism and global trade that radically altered the world forever. It was the first step toward creating the "globalized" world that we live in today.

Why and Where Did It Occur?

Why did merchant capitalism develop in a relative backwater spot in the world at the particular time that it did? Compared to the great civilizations of China, South Asia, and Southwest Asia, Europe in the early Middle Ages lagged far behind in terms of technology and scientific know-how. Earlier, traditional theories attributed the development of merchant capitalism in northwest Europe to such things as Protestant Christianity (Weber's "Protestant work ethic") or European racial superiority. While some still hold Weber's theory to be of explanatory value, nobody still believes that Europeans were somehow "better" or "smarter" than other world civilizations and "invented" capitalism due to this superiority. Instead, most historians today argue that a series of events happened first in Europe, affecting societies there in more drastic ways than others and resulting in a fundamental reordering of European societies and economies.

The most important of these events was most likely the **Black Death**, the Bubonic plague that ravaged Europe from 1340 to 1440. The Black Death struck elsewhere around the world, but nowhere with such far-reaching consequences. Anywhere from one-third to one-half of the population of Europe died during this period. Most of those that died came from the peasant classes, in a feudal society, that part of the population with the lowest caloric intake and the highest susceptibility to such respiratory diseases. This loss had drastic repercussions for European economies because with so much of the peasantry gone, labor was now in very short supply. As a result, those peasants that remained acquired something that they had never possessed before—bargaining power over their aristocratic landlords. Peasants began to demand something for their labor, either payment in kind or money wages. In short, the Black Death precipitated a **crisis of feudalism** in Europe. The ancient feudal organization of labor and production could no longer keep up with the demand for food, especially as populations began to increase rapidly again after the plagues subsided. World-systems analysts argue that the replacement of a feudal organization to societies and economies with a different form of production and exchange based on individual money profit—capitalism—was the solution to this crisis in the feudal order.

Along with the reordering of economies came a fundamental reordering of societies as well, the most important aspect of which was the emergence of a new class of people—a middle class. Because production was now based on profit and competition, those that could produce the most reaped the most profit. This spurred technological innovations, especially in agricultural production. The use of steel plows, the draining of marshlands, and crop rotation schemes, for example, led to higher agricultural surpluses than ever before. This reordering also meant that more and more of the European population did not have to farm because agriculture had become more efficient and more productive. Many people began to move to towns and cities and became shopkeepers, merchants, and artisans (weavers, blacksmiths, millers, tailors, bakers, etc.). Over ensuing generations, this new middle class rose in social, economic, and political importance, and the middle class began to pass on wealth to successive generations. Such dynastic, wealthy urban merchant families came to dominate the social and economic life of coastal towns in northwestern Europe, especially in Holland and England, by the sixteenth and seventeenth centuries. By the late sixteenth century, these powerful urban merchants began to sponsor overseas trading ventures to newly "discovered" tropical regions to supply the new and growing demand for rare, expensive tropical agricultural products by the expanding middle class. **Colonialism**—the political, economic, and social control of tropical peripheral regions by European core powers using coerced labor—was invented by northwestern European urban merchant capitalists to more efficiently supply this demand. It was this new merchant capitalist colonial order that created the European-centered capitalist world-economy with its characteristic tripartite global economic geography of core, semi-periphery, and periphery.

What Changes Did It Engender?

In summary, the development and expansion of merchant capitalism based on long-distance sea trade resulted in the following revolutionary developments:

- The replacement of feudal, agricultural societies with economies dominated by merchant capital interests involved in long-distance sea trade
- The invention and domination of colonialism
- The birth and dominance of a middle class of urban merchant entrepreneurs
- The creation of a capitalist world-economy dominated by a few nation-states in Europe
- The creation of a "core" of relatively high economic and technological development and a "periphery" of relatively low economic and technological development

- The creation of the use of varying labor control systems in the different part of the world-economy: slavery in the periphery, wage labor in the core, and tenant farming in the semi-periphery
- The increased use of nonhuman and non-animal sources of energy; a drastic increase in the amount of energy harnessed per capita, per year
- The initiation of a capitalistic logic in the world-economy; since capitalism rewards innovations that make production cheaper, it engenders constant technological innovation

THE INDUSTRIAL REVOLUTION

What Was It, and Where Did It Occur?

The **Industrial Revolution** represents a third major break with the past with respect to far-reaching societal changes around the world, especially in the core countries of the world-economy during the nineteenth and twentieth centuries; their wealth was built on the backs of economies focused on heavy industry and manufacturing. Most significantly, the Industrial Revolution ushered in vastly different methods and modes of industrial production, systems of labor control, and social relations of production. These changes occurred first in the Midlands of central England beginning in the early- to mid-eighteenth century but spread very quickly to the rest of Europe (Belgium, Holland, France, Germany, and Russia) and North America (especially the northeast United States) by the mid- to late-nineteenth century. The Industrial Revolution ushered in the Machine Age.

The Industrial Revolution radically altered societies and economies in two important ways. First, modes of production were revolutionized with the introduction and application of new labor-saving technologies and machines. The earliest of these new technologies was the steam engine, first put to use in the British Midlands running pumps to remove excess water from coal mines; but, the technology was soon put to use running all types of machines that heretofore had employed human or animal power, such as mills and looms. The first industry to be completely revolutionized by the machine age was the textile industry. Steam engines that spun and wove yarn into textile goods replaced traditional cottage textile industries in the rural countryside of Europe, where such goods had for millennia been produced by hand. The mode of production that came to dominate regions that became industrialized was the urban factory staffed by low-wage, low-skilled workers running steam-driven machines.

Many of these workers were women and children from the rural hinterlands of emerging industrial cities who came to the cities in search of work because traditional ways of making a living were being radically altered. This migration represents the second major change wrought by the Industrial Revolution—a new form of labor control characterized by the factory organization of low-wage, low-skilled laborers. Such laborers lived in housing, often built by the factory owners, very near to the factories in which they worked. Long working hours (production could take place around the clock with the advent of gas lighting and, later, electricity), poor living conditions, and exposure to hazardous environmental pollutants (coal smoke, chemicals) characterized the lives of the earliest factory workers. Workers often performed the same menial tasks hour after hour in cramped and hot conditions. In the United States, the industrialist Henry Ford mastered the factory mode of production and labor control with the innovation of the assembly line, where workers performed the same task hour after hour as cars traveled down an assembly line (this mode of production is often called **Fordism**).

The factory mode of production built around urban factories staffed by low-skilled wage laborers and powered by petroleum-based fuels (first coal, then oil products like gasoline) revolutionized production. The countries that industrialized first, like Great Britain, Germany, and the United States, soon outpaced and outproduced their competitors. Although industrialization came to different countries at different times, the economies of all of the core powers of today were built upon heavy industrial production between the mid-eighteenth century and 1960. Industrialization brought immense wealth and power to these core countries, especially in the early twentieth century when steel production, shipbuilding, and automobile manufacturing became the hallmark of the core economies. Many semi-peripheral areas did not industrialize until the 1960s and 1970s, while large-scale industrialization has yet to appear in most areas of the periphery. The semi-peripheral economies hope that a strong manufacturing and heavy industry base will also bring the same wealth that it brought to the core economies, but it remains to be seen whether this will happen or not.

THE POST-INDUSTRIAL (POST-MODERN) REVOLUTION

The **Post-Industrial Revolution** describes revolutionary changes in societies, economies, and cultures that have taken place since the early 1970s, predominately in the core regions of the world-economy. But, because changes that take place in the core affect all regions of the world-economy, this revolutionary period in which we now live is fundamentally transforming societies, economies, and cultures all over the world. This period has seen the development of new modes of production, the advent of so-called "new information technologies" such as the internet (these have ushered in the "computer age"), and a pronounced global division of labor in the world-economy.

Perhaps the most significant development during this latest revolution is the process of **globalization** in the world-economy, directed from the core by multi-national conglomerates employing rapidly evolving forms of information technology to increasingly expand the scope of *interconnectedness* among the parts of the world-economy. Such interconnectedness has led not only to a fundamental restructuring of the world-economy. This post-industrial or "postmodern" age has also ushered in an era in which people and places all over the world are linked and tied together to a degree never before seen in human history. Rapidly evolving forms of mass communication, faster and cheaper forms of travel between continents, and large-scale international migrations are all in part responsible for such international linkages.

In terms of modes of production, a central feature of the post-industrial era has been a restructuring of the world-economy characterized by globalization and a marked international division of labor. In the core regions of the world-economy, this restructuring involved a move from economies based on heavy industry and manufacturing between World War II and the early 1970s, to service-based economies from the 1970s until the present. Manufacturing jobs and manufacturing-based industries (such as steel production and automobile assembly plants), once the cornerstone of core economies, have increasingly moved to the semi-periphery and, in some instances, to peripheral locations. This process may be called **global outsourcing**, and it has occurred primarily due to lower costs of labor (wages) in semi-peripheral and peripheral locations such as Mexico, Indonesia, Malaysia, and much of Latin America. This geographical outsourcing has led to the movement of manufacturing-based industries and jobs (especially those with high costs of labor, such as textile production and automobile assembly) to such semi-peripheral locations. In the core regions themselves, a new mode of production, called "just-in-time" or **post-Fordist production**, has replaced traditional factory organizations of labor. So-called "blue collar" low-wage and low-skilled jobs have rapidly declined in number with the decline in the number of manufacturing industries. In their place, a new kind of worker has emerged: highly skilled, high-wage labor in which brains rather than brawn matter the most. This is especially true in the new information technologies, such as in software production and computer assembly, which are an increasingly important part of the core economies in the post-industrial era.

In the end, the post-industrial era has led to a reinforcement of the core—semi-periphery—periphery structure of the world-economy and made the differences between them greater than ever before. That is, life in the core for the average person is vastly different than it is in the periphery. Today, the core controls the flow of wealth and information in the post-industrial world-economy. The core contains the nodes, or nerve centers, of the world-economy (places such as New York, London, and Tokyo), and it is here that the largest multi-national companies in the world are located. Core economies are primarily service-based and information-based in nature. The semi-peripheral regions today are the places where much of the world's manufacturing now takes place. Agriculture is still an important part of these economies, especially the production of plantation products for export to the core. A small but expanding service sector is also characteristic of many of the semi-peripheral economies. Peripheral economies remain largely dependent upon traditional subsistence agricultural economies and plantation agriculture for export to the core. The service and manufacturing sectors of the economy in the periphery are both still rather weakly developed.

Finally, **post-modernism** has significantly altered traditional ways of life and forms of artistic expression such as art, literature, music, and poetry, as well as philosophy and other scientific endeavors. These alterations have been most conspicuous in the core regions of the world-economy, but their effects have trickled down to the semi-periphery and periphery as well, albeit to a lesser extent. Post-modern expression is characterized by a lack of faith in absolute truths, a mélange of forms and styles, a rejection of order, and a deconstruction-ist ideology in which traditional ways of articulation are continually questioned. This post-modern "condition" has resulted in a reordering of societies, econo-mies, and modes of production, especially in the core, and is characterized by the following conditions:

- Increasing globalization of the world-economy
- The development of a "frenetic" international financial system
- The development of, and reliance upon, new information technologies
- A world-economy more and more reliant upon the flow of information
- A world-economy that is increasingly *illegible* to the average person; interconnections are so complex that the world is harder to comprehend, global capitalism is harder to "locate"; a world of confused senses and order
- A world that is increasingly *hyper-mobile*; a world-wide informational economy with telecommunication technology as its foundation; a "space of flows" that dominates sense of place; a perception of the world through the medium of information technologies
- A world increasingly effected by *time-space compression*; a marked increase in the pace of life; a seeming collapse of time and space that affects our abilities to grapple with and comprehend the world

KEY TERMS TO KNOW

Neolithic Revolution	Merchant Capitalism	Globalization
Domestication	The Black Death	Global Outsourcing
Independent Invention	"Crisis of Feudalism"	Post-Fordist Production
Culture Hearth	Colonialism	Post-Modernism
Cultural Diffusion	Industrial Revolution	
"God-kings"	Fordism	
Capitalism	Post-Industrial Revolution	

NAME _____   DATE _____

STUDY QUESTIONS

1. What are the primary characteristics of the Neolithic Revolution? When, why, and where did it occur?

_____
_____
_____
_____
_____
_____
_____
_____
_____

2. What are the defining characteristics of the Merchant Capitalist Revolution? When and where did it occur? What fundamental changes in societies and economies and modes of production resulted from this revolution?

_____
_____
_____
_____
_____
_____
_____
_____
_____

3. Define and describe the main characteristics of the Industrial Revolution. When and where did it occur? What revolutionary changes in industrial modes of production did it engender?

_____

_____

_____

_____

_____

_____

_____

_____

4. Define the Post-Industrial Revolution. When and where did it occur? What fundamental changes in societies, economies, and modes of production resulted from this revolution?

_____

_____

_____

_____

_____

_____

_____

_____

_____

FURTHER READING

Hans Bertens, *Literary Theory: The Basics* (New York: Routledge, 2001).

J. M. Blaut, *The Colonizer's Model of the World: Geographical Diffusionism and Eurocentric History* (New York: Guilford Press, 1993).

Fernand Braudel, *Civilization and Capitalism, 15th–18th Century*, Vol. I, *The Structures of Everyday Life* (New York: Harper & Row, 1981).

Carlo Cippola, *The Fontana Economic History of Europe: The Industrial Revolution, 1700–1914* (London: Fontana, 1976).

Phyllis Deane, *The First Industrial Revolution* (Cambridge: Cambridge University Press, 1979).

Jared Diamond, *Guns, Germs, and Steel: The Fates of Human Societies* (New York: W.W. Norton & Co., 1997).

Michel Foucault, *The Order of Things: An Archaeology of the Human Sciences* (New York: Vintage Books, 1994).

Marvin Harris, *Good to Eat: Riddles of Food and Culture* (Long Grove: Waveland Press, 1985).

David Harvey, *The Condition of Postmodernity* (Oxford: Blackwell, 1989).

J. David Hoeveler, Jr., *The Postmodernist Turn: American Thought and Culture in the 1970s* (Lanham: Roman & Littlefield, 1996).

David Landes, *The Unbound Prometheus: Technological Change and Industrial Development in Western Europe from 1750 to the Present* (Cambridge: Cambridge University Press, 1969).

William McNeill, *The Rise of the West: A History of the Human Community* (Chicago: University of Chicago Press, 1963).

Sidney W. Mintz, *Sweetness and Power: The Place of Sugar in Modern History* (New York: Penguin, 1985).

Lewis Mumford, *Technics and Civilization* (San Diego: Harcourt Brace & Co., 1963).

Carl O. Sauer, *Agricultural Origins and Dispersals* (New York: The American Geographical Society, 1952).

Wolfgang Schivelbusch, *Tastes of Paradise: A Social History of Spices, Stimulants, and Intoxicants* (New York: Vintage Books, 1992).

Peter Stearns, *The Industrial Revolution in World History*, 3rd ed. (Boulder: Westview Press, 2007).

Immanuel Wallerstein, *The Modern World-System I: Capitalist Agriculture and the Origins of the European World-Economy in the Sixteenth Century* (San Diego: Academic Press, 1981).

CHAPTER 3

THE CONCEPT OF HUMAN "CULTURE"

In This Chapter:

VARYING DEFINITIONS AND CRITIQUES OF "CULTURE"

Traditional Definitions

Culture is one of those words that many of us often use without thinking very deeply about what it exactly means. In the post-industrial era, punctuated by the so-called "culture wars" and post-modern dialogue, it is often used as a catch-all term to describe attributes relating to such things as race, ethnicity, and gender. Today, *culture* is a highly elusive term that means a lot to some social scientists but nothing at all to others. That is, its meaning and importance are highly debated, and in academia today, it is one of those ideas that is being rigorously critiqued and deconstructed. But, however one might approach or define human culture, there is no denying that the study of how it varies geographically and how it shapes and influences cultural landscapes is central to the field of human geography. It is altogether necessary, then, to have a basic understanding of what culture is, how different academic traditions define it, and how it is expressed in the landscape in different parts of the world-economy.

Although the concept of human culture in its various forms is a central focus of most of the humanities and social sciences, it tends to be defined in different ways by various academic disciplines. Sociology, for example, stresses the codes and values of a group of people. Sociologists would argue that to really know the culture of a group, whether it be an ethnic group or a class of people or an entire society, one must understand the rules of conduct members of that group have agreed upon. These rules of conduct might include laws, social mores and traditions, and codes relating to family and societal structure. Sociologists tend to look at how order is achieved and how society is organized to understand the values and traditions of that society. Anthropology, a discipline defined as the study of human cultures, tends to focus on the everyday ways of life of a group or society. Such ways of life might include linguistic norms, religious ideals, food, dress, music, and political structures. To uncover and understand the cultural values and traditions of a group or society, anthropologists study these ways of life.

While there is a long tradition of debate about the meaning and nature of culture in the academic literature of many of the social sciences, cultural geographers, until recently, have traditionally spent little time defining what culture is. Instead, traditional human and cultural geography in the United States focused on how culture was expressed in the landscapes of places—the landscape, especially its physical manifestations such as houses, fields, settlement patterns, neighborhoods, etc., were "read" and analyzed to uncover clues about the cultural values and traditions of the people that built them. Until post-modern thought began to influence the field in the 1970s, most cultural geographers were content to rely on definitions of culture that sociologists and cultural anthropologists had developed in the twentieth century. For these cultural geographers, then, human culture consists of many aspects of a group or society that, when combined together, results in a distinctive way of life that distinguishes that group or society from others:

- Beliefs (religious beliefs and political ideals, for example)
- Speech (language and linguistic norms and ideals)
- Institutions (such as governmental and legal institutions)
- Technology (skills, tools, use of natural resources)
- Values and Traditions (art, architecture, food, dress, music, etc.)

As such, cultural values and traditions are not biological in nature. Such traditions are learned, not genetically inherited (that is, we are not born with these values), and are passed on from generation to generation through a mutually intelligible language and a common symbol pool or iconography. For cultural geographers, who seek to identify the spatial expression of culture, a **culture region** is an area in which a distinctive way of life (as defined above) is dominant.

The New Cultural Geography

Post-modern thought has had a dramatic effect on the field of cultural geography over the past 20 years, especially in Great Britain and the United States. In what has come to be known as **The New Cultural Geography**, a new generation of scholars is turning upside down traditional notions of culture and its expression on the landscape. Heavily influenced by post-modern literary and philosophical traditions, and by neo-Marxist thought, one of the leading voices in this new movement has gone so far as to argue that culture does not even exist and that we learn little about the nature of the world and its societies by approaching culture in the traditional ways outlined above. Rather, it is argued by the new cultural geographers that what we might call "culture," for lack of a better term is not a thing, but rather a process that shapes values, traditions, and ideals. These processes and their accompanying values and traditions differ significantly, not from society to society or country to country, but from person to person; they are influenced by such things as an individual's class, gender, race, and sexuality. In this line of thought, it follows that our perception of the world is influenced by the same factors, and it is argued that cultural landscapes hold clues to such factors working in society. They can be read, deconstructed, and analyzed in the same way that a literary text can. The cultural landscape, then, is not seen as simply the built environment or the human imprint on the physical landscape. Instead, the New Cultural Geography conceptualizes it as a place or a stage upon which, and within which, societal problems and processes are worked out, especially with respect to struggles relating to class, race, ethnicity, gender, and politics.

CORE-PERIPHERY RELATIONSHIPS

Folk Cultures

Both traditional and post-modern conceptualizations are valuable for a broad understanding of how culture varies around the world. Employing these ideas alongside the core, semi-periphery, periphery model of the world-economy from world-systems analysis, we can understand basic, general differences in ways of life around the world. These basic differences do not translate well down to the local or individual level. To understand the cultural processes at work at such scales, we must analyze cultural processes and patterns at those scales. Here, we are concerned with broad global patterns.

At the global scale, and in a broad sense, we can distinguish between two primary types of culture operating today. At one end of the spectrum are so-called folk cultures. This term describes human societies and cultures that existed in most parts of the world until the Industrial Revolution. At this point, as the core, semi-peripheral, and peripheral areas of the modern world-economy became better defined, a major divergence occurred. Folk cultures remained the norm in the periphery and parts of the semi-periphery, but in the core, and today in some parts of the semi-periphery, cultural values and traditions came to be increasingly modified by "popular" tropes, fads, and ideas (this is discussed in more detail below).

A **folk culture** refers to a way of life practiced by a group that is usually rural, cohesive, and relatively homogeneous in nature regarding traditions, lifestyles, and customs. Such groups and societies are characterized by relatively weak social stratification; goods and tools are handmade according to tradition that is passed on by word of mouth through tales, stories and songs,; and nonmaterial cultural traits (e.g., stories, lore, religious ideals) are more important than material traits (e.g., structures and technologies). The economies of folk societies are most characteristically subsistence in nature—farming or artisan activities are undertaken not to necessarily make a profit, but rather to simply survive—and the markets for such products are usually local or regional in nature. Finally, order in folk cultures is based around the structure of the nuclear family, ancient traditions, and religious ideals. If we define a folk culture by these characteristics (and this is a very conservative definition), then such cultures and societies are practically nonexistent in the core of the world-economy. Instead, they describe most societies that are tribal or "traditional" in nature in the periphery and in some remote, rural parts of the semi-periphery (the Amazon Basin of Brazil, for example, which is part of the semi-periphery). Even so, some folk culture traits almost always persevere even in the post-industrial societies of the core; they are holdovers of our folk cultural roots from hundreds or even thousands of years ago. Some examples would include the popularity of astrology or tarot card reading, the fairy tales that each of us learns as children, and folk songs from long ago that are still passed on today ("Auld Lange Synge" or "Yankee Doodle").

Popular Cultures

While folk cultural traditions dominate most societies in the periphery, the societies of the core and parts of the semi-periphery today are best described by the term *popular culture*. Although some ethnic groups in core regions of the world-economy attempt to live in a traditional or folk manner, or practice a traditional lifestyle, it is nearly impossible for such groups do so in the core because popular culture is so pervasive and far-reaching. For example, even though many Americans see the Amish as a distinctively folk society, closer inspection reveals that, compared to true folk cultures in the periphery, Amish society today is not truly folk in nature. Although most Amish do not use electricity and they do employ rather simple machinery in their agricultural systems, that machinery is mass-produced, material for barns and houses is purchased from retail stores, and their agricultural endeavors are capitalistic, profit-making undertakings.

Compared with folk cultures, **popular cultures** are based in large, heterogeneous societies that are most often ethnically plural, with a concomitant plurality of values, traditions, and ideals. While folk cultures are by definition conservative (that is, resistant to change), popular cultures are constantly changing. This is due to the power and influence of fads and trends that change rapidly and often in core societies, as well as to the dominance and influence of mass communication in the core. While ideas and trends are slow to move from place to place in folk cultures (usually through hierarchical diffusion), they can move around the planet instantaneously by means of mass communication technology (satellites, the internet, television, radio, etc.) in a popular culture (by means of contagious diffusion). This, in fact, is the central defining characteristic of popular cultures— such fast change and quick diffusion is what makes a culture subject to "popular" (read trends and fads) ideas. In the post-modern era, such trends and fads have significantly shaped how people in core societies receive news, what music they listen to, what books they read, what movies they see, what food they eat, and what clothes they wear. In a folk culture, such things are dictated by tradition that has been passed on by word of mouth over many generations.

Other characteristics of popular cultures include the use of material goods that are invariably mass-produced, and societies in which secular institutions (government, the film industry, MTV, multi-national corporations employing advertisements to entice people to buy their products) are of increasing importance in shaping the "look," the landscapes, and ways of life in core societies. The power of such popular fads, trends, and ideas is expressed in the standardized landscapes that are a hallmark of the core and parts of the semi-periphery. That is, popular culture tends to produce standardization that is reproduced *everywhere* in such societies. This can be seen in styles of architecture, music, clothing, dialects, etc., that are the same throughout large, populous societies and over large distances. Currently, the strongest popular culture in the world stems from the United States. Things "American" (music, food, films, styles and the like) affect nearly every place on the planet, including even traditional folk societies in the periphery. Because the diffusion of popular ideas and fads occurs via mass communication, even traditional societies in far corners of the developing world are not immune to the influences of popular culture from the core.

Delimiting and defining the geography of popular culture presents a challenge to human geographers because such cultures tend to produce "placelessness" that challenges unique regional expression. For example, ranch-style homes became popular in the United States in the 1950s. Although the style probably originated in the eastern part of the country, such houses became so popular so fast that they soon could be found everywhere around the country, including Alaska and Hawaii. Another example would be popular music. When a song goes out over the radio or on television, it is heard by millions of people at once, all over the country, or even the world. That song, then, becomes known by millions of people of varying ethnicities, cultures, and nationalities—it has become a song known to millions, not just a few members of a specific tribe or ethnic group, as is the case with a folk song. In this way, popular culture fads and trends are extremely powerful. Popular culture supersedes ethnic and national boundaries, and spreads rapidly across large distances, often at the expense of local or regional folk cultures. Even so, regional expression often still exists in the form of such things as regional dialects, accents, and food preferences, even in societies such as the United States where strong popular cultures predominate. For example, many people in the South today continue to speak English with a strong regional accent even though most people there are exposed to standardized, accent-neutral English in schools and on television news programs and the like.

The post-industrial world-economy of today is punctuated by stark divisions within it. In the previous chapters, we have seen how this plays with respect to vast differences between the core, semi-periphery, and periphery in such things as standards of living, population structure, modes of production, and social relations of production. This chapter has demonstrated that these differences are also seen in the types of cultures operating in the world-economy: popular cultures in the core, folk cultures in the periphery, and a mix of each in the semi-periphery. The following chapters will address a variety of other aspects of culture and argue that these too vary with respect to location in the world-economy.

KEY TERMS TO KNOW

Culture

Culture Region

The New Cultural
   Geography

Folk Culture

Popular Culture

STUDY QUESTIONS

1. How has the field of geography traditionally addressed and defined the concept of culture?

_____

_____

_____

_____

_____

_____

_____

_____

2. How does the New Cultural Geography conceptualize human "culture," and how does this differ from traditional treatments of the subject by human and cultural geographers?

_____

_____

_____

_____

_____

_____

_____

_____

3. What constitutes a folk culture, and where would one most likely find a true folk culture in the present world-economy?

_____

_____

_____

_____

_____

_____

_____

_____

_____

4. In what ways does popular culture differ from folk culture? In what manner does popular culture diffuse from place to place, and where are the effects of popular cultures most pervasive?

_____

_____

_____

_____

_____

_____

_____

_____

_____

FURTHER READING

Jeff Chang and D.J. Kool Herc, *Can't Stop Won't Stop: A History of the Hip-Hop Generation* (New York: Picador, 2005).

Henry Glassie, *Pattern in the Material Folk Culture of the Eastern United States* (Philadelphia: University of Pennsylvania Press, 1968).

Marvin Harris, *Cows, Pigs, Wars, and Witches: The Riddles of Culture* (New York: Vintage Books, 1989).

Marvin Harris, *Theories of Culture in Postmodern Times* (Lanham: AltaMira Press, 1998)

Alan Light, ed., *The Vibe History of Hip-Hop* (New York: Plexus, 1999).

D. W. Meinig, ed., *The Interpretation of Ordinary Landscapes: Geographical Essays* (New York: Oxford University Press, 1979).

Donald Mitchell, *Cultural Geography: A Critical Introduction* (Oxford: Blackwell, 2000).

S. Craig Watkins, *Hip Hop Matters: Politics, Pop Culture, and the Struggle for the Soul of a Movement* (New York: Beacon Press, 2006).

Wilbur Zelinsky, *Exploring the Beloved Country: Geographic Forays into American Society and Culture* (Iowa City: University of Iowa Press, 1994).

CHAPTER 4

THE GEOGRAPHY OF LANGUAGE AND RELIGION

In This Chapter:

Students in an introductory human geography course might wonder why the analysis of the distribution of languages and religions is such a prominent component of most such courses, given that language is the central theme of linguistics and religion is a major theme of philosophy and history. The answer really is very simple: language and religion are the defining cornerstones of human culture (at least as it is traditionally defined) and identity (ethnic and national, or even individual, identity). They are two of the most important characteristics that distinguish human beings from all other animals, given that no other species possesses the capacity for speech or the ability to perceive of one's own mortality in a spiritual sense (at least as far as most biologists know). Many other kinds of animals can communicate with each other, sometimes in very complex ways, but none possesses the capacity for language. Likewise, it is clear that many other species exhibit emotions and feelings, but so far as we know, no others can think and philosophize about what is going to happen to them when they die. So, if a main goal of human geography is to delineate and understand how human cultures vary over space, then it behooves us to know how the two major facets of culture vary over space. That is, a map of religious and linguistic regions is, in many ways, a map of culture regions.

THE CLASSIFICATION AND DISTRIBUTION OF LANGUAGES

Classification of Languages

Language is defined as an organized system of spoken and/or written words, words themselves consisting of symbols or a group of symbols put together to represent either a thing or an idea, depending on the kind of writing system in use. In **syllabic languages**, the symbols that are used (e.g., letters) represent sounds. German, English, Arabic, and Hindi are examples of syllabic languages. **Ideographic languages** employ ideographs as symbols to represent an idea or thing. Examples of ideographic languages include Chinese, Japanese, and Korean. All human beings are biologically "hard-wired" for language. This means not that we are born knowing a language, but rather that we are born with the *ability* to learn a language or languages because it is imbedded in our genetic makeup. The linguist Noam Chomsky calls this "deep structure."

With respect to other forms of animal communication, human language is unique in two primary ways. First, human languages are *recombinant*. This means that words and symbols can be taken out of order in a sentence and recombined to form a different sentence and thus communicate a completely different, or even subtly different, idea. Dogs, for example, are not capable of arranging barks in different orders to communicate extremely intricate ideas. Second, word formation in all human languages is almost completely *arbitrary*. This means that there really is no rhyme or reason about why a certain word, symbol, or ideograph is used to stand for something. There are, of course, exceptions to this rule. One is *sound symbolism*, in which the pronunciation of a word or the shape of an ideograph suggests an image or meaning. For example, many words in English that begin with *gl-* have something to do with sight (glimmer, glow, and glisten). Another exception to this rule is *onomatopoeia*, an instance in which a word sounds like something in nature that it represents (e.g., cuckoo, swish, cock-a-doodle-doo). But, such exceptions are very rare. The vast majority of words in all languages have simply been made up and then passed down over generations, although, to be sure, words and languages change over time.

Roughly 6,700 different languages are in use around the world today. But, the vast majority of these languages are spoken by a relatively small number of people. This means that a relatively small number of languages have thousands or even millions of speakers. Consider the following list of the top ten languages by number of native (mother-tongue) speakers in 2009, according to SIL International, one of the leading organizations that collect and publish linguistic data (www.ethnologue.com):

LANGUAGE	PRIMARY LOCATIONS	NUMBER OF SPEAKERS
Chinese	China	1.213 billion
Spanish	Middle America, Latin America, Spain	329 million
English	North America, British Isles, Australia, New Zealand	328 million
Arabic	Southwest Asia, North Africa, South-Central Asia	221 million
Hindi	India	182 million
Bengali	Bangladesh	181 million
Portuguese	Brazil, Portugal	178 million
Russian	Russia	144 million
Japanese	Japan	122 million
German	Germany, Austria, Switzerland	90 million

Of the nearly 6,700 languages in use today, 389 (about 6%) account for 94% of the world's population. The remaining 94% of languages in the world are spoken by only 6% of the world's population.

Linguists have devised classification schemes that describe and account for similarities and differences between and within different languages. At the broadest level, a **proto-language** describes an ancestral language from which several language families (described below) or languages are descended. No proto-languages are spoken today, but they are theorized to have been in use thousands of years ago. For example, Proto Indo-European was the language theorized to have been spoken in eastern Anatolia (present-day Turkey) and the Caucasus Mountain region 5,000 years ago. These people were the original Indo-Europeans (probably some of the first Caucasians), and the language they developed became the basis for all of the languages linguists classify as Indo-European. If we use the analogy of a tree to represent a group of languages that are linguistically related, then a proto-language is the roots and trunk of the tree.

In this analogy, each branch of the tree represents a **language family**. A language family is a group of languages descended from a single earlier language whose similarity and "relatedness" cannot be the result of circumstance. How do we know that certain languages are related to each other? Linguists employ two main methods to determine linguistic relatedness. One is genetic classification, in which it is assumed that languages have diverged from common ancestor languages (proto-languages), and therefore, languages that diverged from the same proto-language will have inherent similarities. Compare, for example, the following words for "mother" in selected Indo-European languages:

English	*mother*
Dutch	*Moeder*
German	*Mütter*
Irish Gaelic	*mathair*
Hindi	*mathair*
Russian	*mat*
Czech	*matka*
Latin	*mater*
Spanish	*madre*
French	*mére*

It is obvious that all of these words sound very similar to each another. Given the rule that word formation is arbitrary, it is impossible that such strong similarities are the result of mere coincidence, especially given the fact that some of these populations are separated by thousands and thousands of miles. When we add to this list hundreds or thousands of other words that display such similarities, it is clear that these languages have a common ancestor, common linguistic roots. When languages are shown to have a common ancestor, such as those above, they are said to be **cognate languages**.

Reviewing the list above once again, some of the languages clearly have even more commonalities to others in the list. Compare, for example, the even more clearly defined similarity between Latin and Spanish, English and Dutch, and Russian and Czech. These groupings of languages whose commonality is very definite are called **language subfamilies**. Think of these groupings as twigs of larger branches on the language tree, while individual languages are the leaves of the tree. Proceeding even further with respect to similarity, linguists recognize **dialects**. A dialect is defined as a recognizable speech variation *within the same language* that distinguishes one group from another, both of which speak the same language. Sometimes these differences are based on pronunciation alone (the different varieties of English spoken around the world or a Southern or New England accent) and sometimes they are based on slightly different words for the same thing (British English "lorry," American English "truck"). Similarly, **pidgins** are languages that develop from one or more "mother" languages that have highly simplified sentence and grammatical structures compared to the mother languages. When such a language becomes the native language of succeeding generations, it is known as a **creole language**. Most creoles are either English-, French-, or Spanish-based and are spoken in the periphery of the world-economy, in former colonial areas, where two or more groups of people speaking mutually unintelligible languages were forced to communicate with each other during the colonial era.

Political and ethnic fragmentation is characteristic of many former colonial regions in the periphery of the world-economy. In Nigeria, for example, at least 500 different tribal languages are spoken, many of them not even in the same language family. In such places, governments and businesses often make use of a *lingua franca* to carry out official business. A lingua franca refers to a language that is used habitually among people living in close contact with each other whose native tongues are mutually unintelligible. English and French are common lingua francas in much of sub-Saharan Africa, Arabic is the lingua franca of much of North Africa and Southwest Asia, and English can be thought of as the lingua franca of the internet and of air traffic control and airline pilots around the world.

Linguistic Diffusion and Change

Why does the map of world language families look the way it does? What spatial processes have led to the present-day distribution of languages? How do languages change over time and space? In general, cultural diffusion (both hierarchical and relocation diffusion) and geographical isolation over time and space have resulted in the linguistic patterns we observe today. Relocation diffusion on a massive scale since the advent of the capitalist world-economy in the fifteenth century, together with the displacement and subjugation of native populations, has resulted in very large linguistic regions, especially in the Americas.

These two processes (relocation diffusion and displacement) explain the fact that the vast majority of populations in North, South, and Middle America speak one of three languages (all of them Indo-European languages): English, Spanish, and Portuguese. Before Columbian contact, probably as many as 30 million people were living in the Americas, speaking literally hundreds of distinctive languages in at least a dozen different language families. In other words, the linguistic map was highly complicated and extremely diverse. Massive relocation from Europe and the decimation of native populations over a 300-year period resulted in a vastly simplified and less complex linguistic map in the Americas. This is not to say that no Native American languages survive. Many do, but with few exceptions, the number of people who speak these languages is very small compared to the number of English, Spanish, and Portuguese speakers. The colonial era also ushered in a period in which many European languages, such as English, Spanish, Portuguese, and French, acquired many more new speakers in their overseas colonies than they ever had at home. In part, this was a result of the outright extermination of African and Native American languages in the Americas through either severe population decline or cultural subjugation through slavery. In the process, European languages were of course deemed as "superior" to others, and Europeans forced Africans and Native Americans to learn the language of the colonizers. This was the case not only in the Americas, but also in colonial sub-Saharan Africa as well.

The present-day world linguistic map also is the product of centuries of linguistic change over time and space. In the pre-industrial era, for example, migration and spatial isolation and segregation gave rise to separate, mutually unintelligible languages. As populations diverged over time and space, populations became isolated from each other. And, as these migrating populations encountered new natural environments and human societies, they were forced to invent new words to describe new circumstances, places, and things. It has also been shown that languages change naturally in place over time, even in the absence of outside cultural forces such as immigration or hostile invasion. Take, for example, the case of English and how significantly the language changed between the ninth and seventeenth centuries. The Old English of ninth-century Britain (*Beowulf* is the most famous literary example) would hardly be recognizable to most English speakers today. But, 500 years later, due to influences from Latin, French, and Danish, as well as to natural linguistic evolution over time, the language had evolved into the Middle English of Chaucer (*The Canterbury Tales*), a language that most English speakers today can understand. By the seventeenth century, the language had evolved into the Modern English of Shakespeare. As one of the world's most widely spoken languages and as a world-wide lingua franca, English is changing more rapidly today than ever before as it incorporates words from a variety of different cultural sources around the world.

The Distribution of the World's Major Language Families

This section lists the world's major language families and important subfamilies, and maps the distribution of their speakers.

1. **Indo-European Family (386 languages; about 2.5 billion speakers)**
   - Albanian Subfamily—Albania, parts of Yugoslavia and Greece
   - Armenian Subfamily—Armenia
   - Baltic Subfamily—Latvia, Lithuania
   - Celtic Subfamily—parts of western Ireland, Scotland, Wales, Brittany

- Germanic Subfamily—northern and western Europe, Canada, USA, Australia, New Zealand, parts of the Caribbean and Africa
- Greek Subfamily—Greece, Cyprus, parts of Turkey
- Indo-Iranian Subfamily—India, Pakistan, Bangladesh, Afghanistan, Iran, Nepal, parts of Sri Lanka, Kurdistan (Iran, Iraq, Turkey)
- Italic (Romance) Subfamily—France, Spain, Portugal, Italy, Romania, Brazil, parts of western and central Africa, parts of the Caribbean, parts of Switzerland
- Slavic Subfamily—eastern Europe, southeastern Europe, parts of south-central Asia

2. **Sino-Tibetan Family (272 languages; about 1.1 billion speakers)**
   - Chinese Subfamily—China, Taiwan, Chinese communities around the world
   - Tibeto-Burman Subfamily—Tibet, Myanmar (Burmese), parts of Nepal and India

3. **Austronesian Family (1,212 languages; 269 million speakers)**
   - Formosan Subfamily—parts of Taiwan
   - Malayo-Polynesian Subfamily—Madagascar, Malaysia, Philippines, Indonesia, New Zealand (Maori), Pacific Islands (e.g., Hawaii, Fiji, Samoa, Tonga, Tahiti)

4. **Afro-Asiatic Family (338 languages; 250 million speakers)**
   - Semitic Subfamily—North Africa (Arabic), Israel (Hebrew), Ethiopia (Amharic), Middle East
   - Cushitic Subfamily—Ethiopia, Kenya, Eritrea, Somalia, Sudan, Tanzania
   - Chadic Subfamily—Chad, parts of Nigeria, Cameroon
   - Omotic Subfamily—Ethiopia
   - Berber Subfamily—parts of Morocco, Algeria, Tunisia

5. **Niger-Congo Family (1,354 languages; 206 million speakers)**
   - Benue-Congo Subfamily—central and southern Africa
   - Kwa Subfamily—bulge of west Africa
   - Adamaw-Ubangi Subfamily—northern part of central Africa
   - Gur Subfamily—between Mali and Nigeria
   - Atlantic Subfamily—extreme western part of the bulge of west Africa
   - Mande Subfamily—western part of the bulge of west Africa

6. **Dravidian Family (70 languages; 165 million speakers)**
   - Four Subfamilies—southern India, parts of Sri Lanka, parts of Pakistan

7. **Japanese Family (12 languages; 126 million speakers)**

8. **Altaic Family (60 languages; 115 million speakers)**
   - Turkic Subfamily—Turkey, Uzbekistan, Turkmenistan, Kazakhstan, Azerbaijan, eastern Russia (Siberia)
   - Mongolian Subfamily—Mongolia, parts of adjoining areas of Russia and China
   - Tungusic Subfamily—Siberia, parts of adjoining areas of China

9. **Austro-Asiatic Family (173 languages; 75 million speakers)**
   - Mon-Khmer Subfamily—Vietnam, Cambodia, parts of Thailand and Laos
   - Munda Subfamily—parts of northeast India

10. **Tai Family (61 languages; ca. 75 million speakers)**
    - Tai Subfamily—Thailand, Laos, parts of China and Vietnam

11. **Korean Family (1 language; 60 million speakers)**

12. **Nilo-Saharan Family (186 languages; 28 million speakers)**
    - Nine Subfamilies—southern Chad, parts of Sudan, Uganda, Kenya

13. **Uralic Family (33 languages; 24 million speakers)**
    - Finno-Ugric Subfamily—Estonia, Finland, Hungary, parts of Russia
    - Samoyedic Subfamily—parts of northern Russia (Siberia)

14. **Amerindian Languages (985 languages; ca. 20 million speakers)**
    - As many as 50 different language families, hundreds of subfamilies
    - North America = ca. 500,000 speakers; 150 languages (top languages = Navajo and Aleut)
    - Central America = ca. 7 million speakers; (top language = Nahuatl)
    - South America = ca. 11 million speakers; (top language = Quechua)

15. **Caucasian Family (38 languages; 7.8 million speakers)**
    - Four Subfamilies—Georgia, surrounding region on western shore of the Caspian Sea

16. **Miao-Yao Family (15 languages; 5.6 million speakers)**
    - Southern China, northern Laos (Hmong), northeast Myanmar

17. **Indo-Pacific Family (734 languages; 3.5 million speakers)**
    - The most linguistically complex place on earth—Papua New Guinea and surrounding islands

18. **Khoisan Family (37 languages; 300,000 speakers)**
    - Three Subfamilies—parts of Namibia, Botswana, Republic of South Africa

19. **Australian Aborigine (262 languages; ca. 30,000 speakers)**
   - Only five languages have over 1,000 speakers
   - At time of European contact, 28 language families, 500 languages spoken by over 300,000 people

20. **Language Isolates (296 languages; ca. 2 million speakers)**
   - Languages that have not been conclusively shown to be related to any other language; some examples are:
     - Basque (Euskara)—southern France, northern Spain
     - Nahali—5,000 speakers in southwest Madhya Pradesh in India
     - Ainu—island of Hokkaido, Japan; now probably extinct
     - Kutenai—less than 200 speakers in British Columbia and Alberta

THE CLASSIFICATION AND DISTRIBUTION OF RELIGIONS

Classification of Religions

Together with language, religion is a human characteristic that distinguishes us from every other animal species on the planet. As with language, we are also most likely biologically "hard-wired" with the capacity for abstract thought about spiritual matters, our own mortality, and the nature of the universe and our place in it. We are born with these capacities, but not with a certain set of beliefs concerning these things—these beliefs are learned. By definition, a **religion** is a system of either formal (written down and codified in practice) or informal (oral traditions passed from generation to generation) beliefs and practices relating to the sacred and the divine. Religion helps us answer questions such as: Who am I? Why am I here? What is my purpose in life? What is my place in the universe? What will happen to me when I die?

Every human being ponders these questions because we have the biological capacity to think about and philosophize about such things. Human religions attempt to answer such questions through systems of beliefs, practices, and worship. As the answers to these questions vary, so do religious belief systems; as the answers to these questions vary from place to place, to a large extent, so does human culture. As is the case with human languages, literally thousands of religions are practiced around the world today. In most of the peripheral regions of the world-economy, there are as many religions as there are ethnic groups, and they can vary substantially over relatively short distances. For human geographers, religion is an extremely important aspect of the cultural landscape because religious beliefs and customs have a significant physical manifestation in the form of religious structures. Although religious practices, beliefs, and traditions vary substantially around the world, most religions share the following characteristics:

- Belief in one or many supernatural authorities
- A shared set of religious symbols (iconography)

- Recognition of a transcendental order—offers a divine reason for existence and an explanation of the inexplicable
- Sacraments (prayer, fasting, baptism, initiation, etc.)
- Enlightened or charismatic leaders (priests, shaman, prophets)
- Religious taboos
- Sacred structures (temples, shrines, cathedrals, mosques, etc.)
- Sacred places (pilgrimage sites, holy cities, etc.)
- Sacred texts

Human religions can be divided into two broad categories and two narrower sub-categories. At the broadest level, we can distinguish between monotheistic and polytheistic religions. **Polytheistic religions** involve a belief in many supernatural (that is, not of this world) beings that control or influence some aspect of the natural or human world. The vast majority of human religions are polytheistic in nature, numbering in the thousands. Such religions usually, but not always, have a very small geographic distribution, often coinciding with tribal or ethnic boundaries. For most of human history, polytheistic belief systems have been by far the most common. **Monotheistic religions** appeared on the human stage quite late, probably not until around 1,500 B.C.E. Monotheism involves the belief in one omnipotent, omniscient, supernatural being who created the universe and everything in it, and thus controls and influences all aspects of the natural and human world. There are in effect only three monotheistic religions today: Judaism, Christianity, and Islam. In terms of number of adherents and believers, however, two of these (Christianity and Islam) have over one billion adherents each. That is, out of a total world population of around 7 billion, fully one-third are either Christians or Muslims. The geographic boundaries of Christian and Islamic beliefs, then, do not coincide with political boundaries but rather supersede and overlap them. We can account for such distributions in much the same way that we can account for the very large distribution of Indo-European speakers around the world: relocation diffusion on a massive scale during the colonial era, and the acquisition of new members either by force or through missionary activities.

We can also identify two sub-categories of religions. First, **ethnic religions** are those in which membership is either by birth (one is "born into" the religion) or by adopting a certain complex ethnic lifestyle, which includes a certain religious belief system. That is, an ethnic religion is the religious belief system of a specific ethnic or tribal group and is unique to that group. Most (but not all) of these kinds of religions are polytheistic in nature and have very small geographical distributions, sometimes no larger than a village or group of villages. These religions, therefore, have very strong territorial or ethnic group identity. In most such religions, there is no distinction made between one's ethnic identity (i.e., one's culture) and one's religion: one's religion *is* one's culture. Examples of ethnic religions include Judaism, Hinduism, and various tribal belief systems that are ubiquitous throughout the periphery of the world-economy. Second, **universalizing religions** are those in which membership is open to anyone who chooses to make a solemn commitment to that religion, regardless of class or ethnicity. Membership in these religions is usually relatively easily obtained, and usually involves some sort of public declaration of one's allegiance to the belief system (baptism, for example). Universalizing religions are also distinguished by the fact that they are often characterized by strong evangelic overtones in which members are admonished to spread the faith to nonbelievers. For these reasons, universalizing religions have very large geographic distributions that cover vast regions of the world, the boundaries of which overlap the political boundaries of individual states. There are only three universalizing religions: Christianity, Islam, and Buddhism, although Buddhism rarely carries with it evangelic activities and therefore has a much smaller distribution than Christianity and Islam.

Finally, it should be noted that the influence of popular culture and post-modern thought and philosophies, especially in core regions of the world-economy, have significantly influenced the growth of secularism. **Secularism** refers to an indifference to, or outright rejection of, a certain belief system or religious belief in general. In its extreme, such "beliefs" may become like a religion. It is increasingly characteristic of many post-industrial societies, and thus influences core societies more than any other societies around the world. At least one-fifth of the world's population, by this definition, is secular, and this figure is even higher in parts of northern and western Europe, where the figure approaches 70 percent in some instances.

A Comparative Approach to Understanding the World's Religions

In his recent book *God is Not One*, the noted religious scholar Stephen Prothero employs a four-part comparative model as a starting point for understanding the world's major religious belief systems and for contextualizing their similarities and differences. Prothero argues that each religion's theology and system of beliefs identify and articulate four primary concerns:

1. A *central problem* with which the theology and belief system is chiefly concerned

2. A *primary solution* to this problem, which in most cases functions as the primary goal of the religion

3. A *technique or set of techniques* for achieving this solution/goal

4. An *exemplar or exemplars* who demonstrate a path from problem to solution

As we approach a comparative analysis of the world's major religions, we will employ this useful framework.

Attributes and Distributions of the World's Major Religions

This section lists the world's major religions, identifies their major characteristics, and maps the distribution of their adherents.

1. **Hinduism (ca. 740 million adherents concentrated in India, Nepal, and Sri Lanka)**
   - One of the world's oldest extant religions
   - The ethnic religion of the Hindustanis
   - Hearth in the Indus Valley ca. 1500 BC, then spread to India, Nepal, Sri Lanka, and parts of SE Asia
   - Beliefs and practices:
     - A common doctrine of *karma*, one's spiritual ranking, and *samsara*, the transfer of souls between humans and/or animals
     - A common doctrine of *dharma*, the ultimate "reality" and power that governs and orders the universe
     - The soul repeatedly dies and is reborn, embodied in a new being
     - One's position in this life is determined by one's past deeds and conduct
     - The goal of existence is to move up in spiritual rank through correct thoughts, deeds and behavior, in order to break the endless cycle and achieve *moksha*, eternal peace
     - Life in all forms is an aspect of the divine—hundreds of gods, each controlling an aspect of the natural world or human behavior
     - One need not "worship" a god or gods
   - **The Caste System**—a social consequence of the Hindu belief system
     - The social and economic class into which one is born is an indication of one's personal status.
     - In order to move up in caste, one must conform to the rules of behavior for one's caste in this life.
     - This thus highly limits social mobility.
   - Sacred texts
     - The *Rig Vedas*, hymns composed by the Indo-Aryans after the invasion of the Punjab; the oldest surviving religious literature in the world, written in Sanskrit
     - *Brahmanas*, theological commentary, defined different castes
     - *Upanishads*, defines karma and nirvana, etc.
   - Cultural landscapes
     - Shrines, village temples, holy places, and rivers (the Ganges), pilgrimage sites and routes

© Melanie Vollmert, 2012. Used under license from Shutterstock, Inc.

The Problem:
- *Samsara*
- The endless cycle of life, death, and rebirth
- "Wandering on" or "flowing"

The Solution(s):
- *Moksha*
  - "Release"
  - Spiritual liberation
  - The freeing of the soul from the bondage to reincarnation
- *Kama*
  - "Sensual pleasure"
- *Artha*
  - Wealth and power
- *Dharma*
  - "Duty"

The Technique(s):
- *Yogas* ("disciplines")
  - *Karma Yoga* (the discipline of ritual action)
  - *Jnana Yoga* (the discipline of wisdom)
  - *Bhakti Yoga* (the discipline of devotion)

The Exemplar(s):
  - *Gurus* ("teachers")
  - Holy men and women
  - Ancient Sanskrit holy texts (the *Vedas*; the *Sutras*; the *Bhagavad Gita*, the *Upanishads*)

2. Buddhism (ca. 300 million concentrated in East and Southeast Asia)

- Founded by Gautama Siddhartha in the sixth century B.C.E. in northeast India
- Diffusion was mainly to China and Southeast Asia by monks and missionaries
- The primary religion in Tibet, Mongolia, Myanmar, Vietnam, Korea, Thailand, Cambodia, Laos; mixed with native faiths in China and Japan
- A universalizing religion
- Beliefs and practices:
  - Retains the Hindu concept of *karma*, but rejects the caste system
  - More of a moral philosophy than a formal religion
  - The ultimate objective is to reach nirvana by achieving perfect enlightenment
  - The road to enlightenment, Buddha taught, lies in the understanding of the four "noble truths": 1. to exist is to suffer, 2. we desire because we suffer, 3. suffering ceases when desire is destroyed, 4. the destruction of desire comes through knowledge or correct behavior and correct thoughts (the "eight-fold path")
- Sects:
  - Theravada (Sri Lanka, Myanmar, Thailand, Laos, Cambodia)
  - Mahayana (Vietnam, Korea, Japan, China, Mongolia)
  - Zen (Japan)
  - Lamaism (Tibet)
- Cultural landscapes:
  - Shrines and temples
  - Holy locations where the Buddha taught

The Buddhist World-View

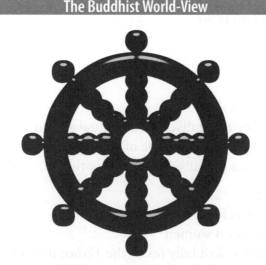

© Georgios Kollidas, 2012. Used under license from Shutterstock, Inc.

The Problem:
- *Dukkha*
  - "Suffering"
  - The undesirable "wandering" from rebirth to rebirth
  - Desiring something other than "what it is"

The Solution(s):
- *Nirvana*
  - "Blowing out" [of suffering]
  - "Awakening"

The Technique(s):
- Understanding of the Four Noble Truths
- The Eightfold Path (ethical conduct; mental discipline; wisdom)
- *Dharma* (understanding things as they really are)
- Meditation
- Chanting

The Exemplar(s):
- *Arhats* (Theravada monastic tradition)
- *Bodhisattvas* (Mahayana "greater vehicle" tradition)
- *Lamas* (Vajrayana "guru/teacher" tradition)

3. **Chinese Faiths (ca. 300 million adherents in China)**
   - Two main forms: Confucianism and Taoism, both date from the sixth century B.C.E.
   - The goal of both is moral harmony within each individual, which leads to political and social harmony.
   - Chinese religion combines elements of Buddhism, Animism, Confucianism, and folk beliefs into one "great religion"; each element services a different component of the self.
   - The Taoist approach to life is embodied in the Yin/Yang symbol; stresses the oneness of humanity and nature; people are but one part of a larger universal order.
   - Confucianism is really a political and social philosophy that became a blueprint for early Chinese civilization; it teaches the moral obligation of people to help each other, that the real meaning of life lies in the here and now, not in a future abstract existence; Kong Fu Chang taught that the secret to social harmony is empathy between people.

© casejustin, 2012. Used under license from Shutterstock, Inc.

The Problem(s):
- Chaos
- Disharmony
- Disorder

The Solution(s):
- Order
- Self-cultivation
- Social Harmony through "Correct" Relations with other Human Beings

The Technique(s):
- Education
- The Study of Ancient Classic Texts
- Learning and Practicing Proper Etiquette and Rituals
- Practicing the "Five Virtues" (human-heartedness; justice; propriety; wisdom; faithfulness)

The Exemplar(s):
- Confucius
- *Junzi* ("exemplary persons")

© J0v43, 2012. Used under license from Shutterstock, Inc.

The Problem(s):

- "Lifelessness"
    - A life that is not fully enjoyed
    - Blind adherence to social conventions
    - Not living life "to its fullest"
    - To be led around by the noose of social conventions and ritual propriety is to be alienated from oneself, from other people, and from the natural environment around us
    - The dictates of social convention, moral rules, formal education, ritual prescriptions
    - All of this destroys social and natural harmony and keeps us from "flourishing" in the way that all living things are meant to

The Solution(s):

- Human "Flourishing"
    - "Nurturing" one's life
    - A vital and genuine life
    - Living life to the fullest
    - In the end, "physical immortality" in this world
    - Living in harmony with the natural rhythms of the Tao (the life force which governs the universe)

The Technique(s):

- Returning to the creativity of the Tao
- Preserving and circulating one's *qi* ("vital energy")
- Balancing one's yin and yang

- "Sitting and forgetting"
- "Free and easy wandering"
- Dietary regimes; breath control; visualization exercises; purification rites; meditation techniques; physical exercises

The Exemplar(s):
- Early Taoist sages (Lao Tzu, for example)
- Taoist texts (*Tao Te Ching*)

4. **Judaism (ca. 18 million adherents mainly in North America and Israel)**
   - The ethnic religion of the Hebrews
   - The oldest religion west of the Indus (ca. 1,500 B.C.E.)
   - Founder regarded as Abraham (the patriarch)
   - Sacred text = the Torah (the five books of Moses)
   - Beliefs and practices:
     - God is the creator of the universe, is omnipotent, but yet merciful to those who "believe" in Him.
     - God established a special relationship with the Jews, and by following his law, they would be special witnesses to His mercy.
     - Emphasis is on ethical behavior and careful, ritual obedience.
     - Among the traditional, almost all aspects of life are governed by strict religious discipline.
     - The Sabbath and other holidays are marked by special observances and public worship.
     - The basic institution is the Synagogue, led by a rabbi chosen by the congregation.
   - Cultural landscapes:
     - Synagogues
     - Sacred sites (e.g., the Wailing Wall, Jerusalem, sites of miracles, etc.)

The Judaic World-View

The Problem:
- Exile (from God)
  - "Distance" from God and where we "ought" to be
  - In both a literal and metaphorical sense
  - A "chronic" problem in Judaic thought

The Solution:
- Return
  - A return back to God and to our "true" home (both literally and metaphorically)
  - The completion of a long journey, from Paradise to desert wilderness, to the New Jerusalem
  - To make things ready and to make things "right"

The Technique(s):
- To Remember
  - To remember the story of one's people and to tell that story;
- To Obey
  - To obey God's law

The Exemplar(s):
- The Patriarchs
  - Abraham, Noah, Moses, Elijah, Esther, among others

5. **Christianity (ca. 1.6 billion adherents worldwide, but especially in Europe, North America, Middle and South America)**
   - A universalizing religion
   - A revision of Judaic belief systems
   - Founder regarded as Jesus, a Jewish preacher believed to be the savior of a sinful humanity promised by God; his main message was that salvation was attainable by all who believed in God (died ca. 30 C.E.)
   - Sacred text = the Bible; Old Testament is based on the Hebrew Torah and is the story of the Jews; New Testament is based on the life of Jesus and his teachings
   - Mission: conversion by evangelism through the offering of the message of eternal life and hope
   - Reform movements:
     - Split in the fifth century between the western church at Rome (Catholicism) and the eastern church at Constantinople (Orthodoxy)
     - Protestant Reformation in the fifteenth and sixteenth centuries, led mainly by northern Europeans over moral and political issues

- Protestantism took hold in northern Europe and spread to North America, Australia and New Zealand
- Cultural landscapes:
  - Churches, cathedrals, graveyards, iconography
  - Sacred sites (e.g. Marian apparition pilgrimage sites)

The Christian World-View

© vladmark, 2012. Used under license from Shutterstock, Inc.

The Problem:
- Sin

The Solution:
- Salvation
- Redemption

The Technique(s):
- Some combination of faith and good works
- Practicing the sacraments of the faith

The Exemplar(s):
- The Saints (Roman Catholicism and Eastern Orthodoxy)
- "Ordinary" People of Faith (Protestantism)

6. **Islam (ca. 1 billion adherents worldwide, but especially in North Africa, Southwest Asia, South-Central Asia, Indonesia, Malaysia)**
   - Founder: Muhammad ("Prophet"), born 571 C.E.; believed to have received the last word of God (Allah) in Mecca in 613 C.E.
   - Diffusion: rapidly throughout Arabia, SW Asia, North Africa, then to South and Southeast Asia
   - Organization: theoretically, the state and the religious community are one in the same, administered by a caliph; in practice, it is a loose confederation of congregations united by tradition and belief
   - A universalizing religion
   - Sacred Text: the Koran—the sayings of Muhammad, believed to be the word of God
   - Divisions: two major sects—Sunni (Orthodox) and Shi'a (Fundamentalist); Shiites mainly in Iran and parts of Iraq and Afghanistan; Sunni are the majority worldwide
   - Beliefs: mainly a revision of both Judaic and Christian beliefs; those who repent and submit ("Islam") to God's rules can return to sinlessness and have everlasting life; religious law as revealed in the Koran is civil law; smoking, gambling and alcohol are forbidden
   - The faithful are admonished to practice the five "**pillars of Islam**"
     - Public profession of faith
     - Daily ritualistic prayer five times per day
     - Almsgiving
     - Fasting during daylight hours during Ramadan
     - A pilgrimage to Mecca at least once in one's lifetime if physically and economically possible
   - Cultural landscapes:
     - Mosques, minarets, religious schools, iconography

The Islamic World-View

The Problem(s):

- Pride
- Disobedience (to God)
- The Fallacy of "Self-Sufficiency" ("the idol of the self")

The Solution(s):

- Submission (to God and God's laws)
- The Achievement of Having a "Soul at Peace" in This Life and the Next

The Technique(s):

- A Combination of Faith and Good Works
- Practicing the "Five Pillars" of the Faith
  - Public profession of the faith
  - Daily prayer
  - Charity
  - Fasting
  - Pilgrimage (to Mecca)

The Exemplar(s):

- Mohammed
- *Imams*
- Many People of "Ordinary" Faith

7. **Sikhism (ca. 25 million adherents worldwide, but concentrated in northwest India, especially the Punjab)**
   - Founder: Guru Nanak (1469–1539) and nine successive Gurus ("teachers")
   - A monotheistic, universalizing religion
   - A Sikh is a "disciple" of God who follows the teachings of the ten Gurus
   - The last Guru died in 1708
   - Beliefs:
     - There is only one God who is creator, sustainer, and destroyer of all life.
     - The same God for all people of all religions.
     - God cannot take human form.
     - The goal of one's life is to break the cycle of death and rebirth and to "merge" with God ("salvation").
     - Salvation may be achieved by overcoming the five cardinal vices (lust, anger, greed, worldly attachment; pride).
     - An emphasis is placed on daily devotion to God.
     - Rejection of all forms of "blind" worship (fasting, yoga, pilgrimage, religious vegetarianism, etc.).
     - Devotees must live "in the world" but keep a "pure" mind.
     - A rejection of all distinctions based around caste, creed, race, gender; equality of women is especially stressed.
     - A stress is placed on charity and community service.

- The Gurus preached a message of love, compassion, and understanding for all human beings and criticized the "blind rituals" of Hindus and Muslims.
- Practices:
  - The very devout decry all forms of violence and undergo a baptism ceremony, after which they become members of a special order; membership in this order requires strict adherence to a Code of Conduct and a prescribed physical appearance (hair is not cut; the wearing of turbans by men; the carrying of a ceremonial sword).
  - Sikhism does not have priests; all Sikhs are considered to be "custodians" of the faith's sacred text.
- Sacred Text:
  - The *Guru Granth Sahib*; this text itself is considered to be the leader of the faith; it was written by the ten Gurus and numerous other authors.
- Cultural Landscapes:
  - The "Gurdwara" (temple); a "Gurdwara" is a structure in which the *Guru Granth Sahib* has been installed; each temple has a community kitchen which serves free meals to people of all faiths;
  - The most significant historical religious center is the Golden Temple at Amritsar, in the state of Punjab in northwest India; it is an inspirational and historic center but not, necessarily, a place of religious pilgrimage

The Sikh World-View

© Nicolas Raymond, 2012. Used under license from Shutterstock, Inc.

The Problem(s):
- Separation from the Divine ("God")
    - This separation comes from giving in to our vices (lust, anger, greed, worldly attachment; pride).
    - This separation results in an endless cycle of death and rebirth in this world.

The Solution(s):
- Salvation
- Becoming One with the Divine ("God")
    - "Merging" with God by breaking the cycle of death and rebirth in this world

The Technique(s):
- Following the Teachings of the Gurus
    - Overcoming the five cardinal vices
    - Love and compassion for all people
    - A rejection of forms of "blind ritual"
    - A rejection of distinctions based on nationality, creed, race, sex, gender, and class

The Exemplar(s):
- Guru Nanak and the Nine Successive Gurus

KEY TERMS TO KNOW

Language	Dialect	Ethnic Religions
Syllabic Languages	Pidgin Language	Universalizing Religions
Ideographic Languages	Creole Language	Secularism
Proto-Language	*Lingua Franca*	The Caste System
Language Family	Religion	The "Pillars of Islam"
Cognate Languages	Polytheistic Religion	
Language Sub-Family	Monotheistic Religion	

STUDY QUESTIONS

1. Why are language and religion important in understanding the distribution of world culture regions?

_____

_____

_____

_____

_____

_____

_____

_____

2. Compare and contrast ethnic and universalizing religions. What are the distinguishing characteristics of each and how do they differ in terms of geographic distribution of adherents?

_____

_____

_____

_____

_____

_____

_____

_____

_____

EXERCISES

1. Using an atlas and one of the blank outline maps of the world on the following pages, create your own map of the distribution of the world's major language families.

2. Using an atlas and the other blank outline map, create your own map of the distribution of adherents of the world's major religions.

Blank Outline Map of the World

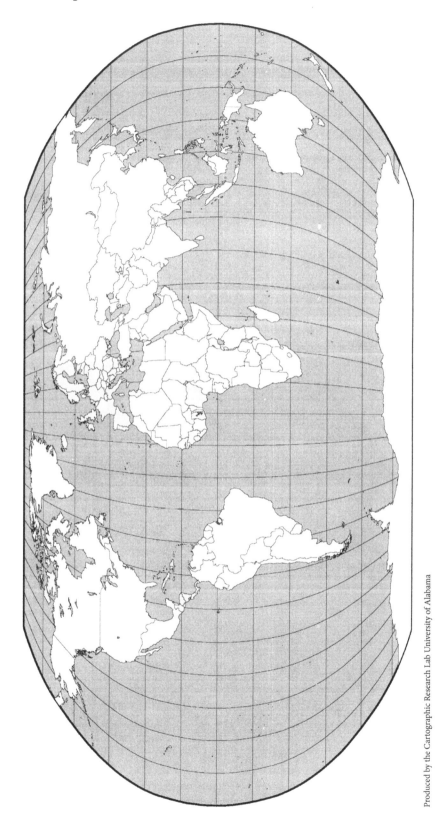

Produced by the Cartographic Research Lab University of Alabama

Blank Outline Map of the World

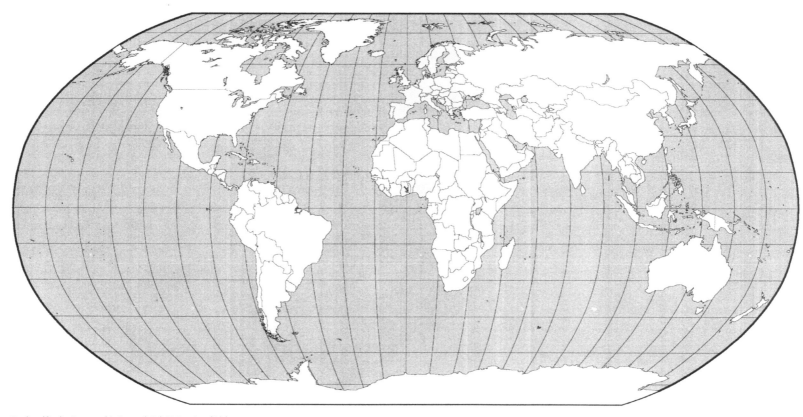

Produced by the Cartographic Research Lab University of Alabama

FURTHER READING

Melvyn Bragg, *The Adventure of English: The Biography of a Language* (London: Hodder & Stoughton, 2003).

Noam Chomsky, *On Language* (New York: New Press, 1998).

David Crystal, *The Cambridge Encyclopedia of Language*, 2nd ed. (Cambridge: Cambridge University Press, 1997).

Mircea Eliade, *The Sacred and the Profane: The Nature of Religion* (San Diego: Harvest Books, 1957).

Susan Tyler Hitchcock, *Geography of Religion: Where God Lives, Where Pilgrims Walk* (Washington: National Geographic Society, 2004).

William James, *The Varieties of Religious Experience* (New York: Penguin, 1958).

M. Paul Lewis, ed., *Ethnologue: Languages of the World*, 16th ed. (Dallas: SIL International, 2009).

Chris Park, *Sacred Worlds: An Introduction to Geography and Religion* (London: Routledge, 1994).

Steven Pinker, *The Language Instinct: How the Mind Creates Language* (New York: Harper Collins, 1995).

Stephen Prothero, *God is Not One: The Eight Rival Religions that Run the World* (New York: HarperOne, 2010).

Ninian Smart, ed., *Atlas of the World's Religions* (Oxford: Oxford University Press, 2009).

Huston Smith, *The World's Religions*, 50th Anniversary Edition (New York: HarperOne, 2009).

Roger W. Stump, *Boundaries of Faith: Geographical Perspectives on Religious Fundamentalism* (Lanham: Rowman & Littlefield, 2000).

Roger W. Stump, *The Geography of Religion: Faith, Place, and Space* (Lanham: Rowman & Littlefield, 2008).

Nicholas Wade, *The Faith Instinct: How Religion Evolved and Why it Endures* (New York: Penguin, 2009).

WEB SITES

Ethnologue (**www.ethnologue.org**)

Sacred Sites: Places of Peace and Power (**www.sacredsites.com**)

Sacred Destinations (**www.sacred-destinations.com**)

SIL International (**www.sil.org**)

THE GEOGRAPHY OF WORLD POPULATION

In This Chapter:

In Chapters 1 and 2, we outlined the development, structure, and geography of the present-day capitalist world-economy. These chapters argued that the tripartite structure of the world-economy (core, semi-periphery, and periphery) is a useful model for understanding the world's human geography. The two previous chapters were mainly concerned with cultural issues and how cultures, in a broad sense, vary from core to periphery. The remaining chapters address in greater detail how the geography of the world-economy varies with respect to social and economic factors such as population, political structure, and economies. We begin in this chapter with how the human population varies across the planet, especially regarding distributions, structures, and core-periphery relationships. The news media and various international organizations often remind us that our world confronts population "problems" today. Invariably, these problems are presented as relating to either overpopulation or how the growing world population affects the supply and use of various natural resources. If there are so-called problems related to population, what are they? Do such issues vary between the core and periphery? How do the structures of populations differ in the zones of the world-economy? How is population distributed around the world? These questions are addressed in this chapter.

WORLD POPULATION DISTRIBUTION

If we examine a map of global population distribution, one of the first things that is readily apparent is that the world's population is not evenly distributed. While some regions are very densely populated (Europe and much of Asia, for example), large parts of the earth (such as the arctic regions, Australia, and Siberia) are very lightly populated. In general, if indeed problems relating to overpopulation exist, those problems are not found everywhere around the world; it is not that there are too many people on the planet (that is a value judgment), but that there are too many people in certain places. The densest population clusters tend to be located in two main types of natural environments around the world. The first is the fertile river valleys of the tropics and subtropics, and the second is the coastal plains of the mid-latitudes, which generally are temperate regions. More precisely, we can identify four major concentrations of population:

- East Asia (China, the Koreas, Vietnam, and Japan)
- South Asia (India, Pakistan, and Bangladesh)
- Europe (The British Isles to western Russia)
- North America (Boston to Washington, D.C.; West Coast)

Roughly 75 percent of the world's population lives in these four areas; four out of ten people in the world live in just two: East and South Asia. Other smaller concentrations of dense populations occur on the island of Java (part of Indonesia), the Nile Valley of Egypt, central Mexico, and southeastern South America (southern Brazil and eastern Argentina).

FACTORS IN WORLD POPULATION

Density

We have described the way populations "look," the way they are structured and their rates of growth, and how that varies significantly between the core and the periphery. It is possible to compare and contrast different populations by comparing various statistics (examples of these statistics for various countries are listed in Table 1.1). One of the most elementary of these factors is population density. Density can be measured as **crude population density**, the total number of people per unit area of land in a place or region, or as **physiologic population density**, the total number of people per unit area of *arable* (agriculturally productive) land. The latter is actually a more telling figure because it measures the density of populations with respect to how much of the land on which they are living is productive enough to produce enough food for that population. When the difference between a country's crude and physiologic densities is very large, it is a sure sign that that country has considerable marginally productive agricultural areas. This can be observed in the following list:

COUNTRY	CRUDE DENSITY/KM²	PHYSIOLOGIC DENSITY/KM²
Japan	862	6,637
Bangladesh	2,124	3,398
Egypt	142	7,101
Netherlands	1,041	4,476
USA	67	335

Growth Rates

A second method for comparing populations is by examining population growth rates.. Since the Industrial Revolution, the world's population has been growing at an exponential rate (2, 4, 8, 16, 32, 64 —). Currently, the world rate of natural increase is about 1.8 percent per annum. This means that 1.8 percent of the current population is being added each year. This figure translates into a current **doubling rate** of 40 years, but this doubling rate will decrease with added population each year. Given this growth rate, the world's population will exceed 7 billion by 2012. It is clear that peripheral populations are growing at a much faster rate than those in the core and semi-periphery. That is, on a broad global scale, direct correlation exists between economic "development" and population growth rates:

COUNTRY	RATE OF NATURAL INCREASE	DOUBLING TIME
Poland	0.5%	141 years
Australia	0.75%	94 years
China	1.5%	46 years
Kenya	4.0%	17 years

Structure

A third way of comparing populations around the world is by observing differences in the structure of populations. By structure, we mean the relative number of men and women in different age cohorts in a population. A population's structure is most clearly seen by constructing a **population pyramid** that charts both male and female populations in five-year age cohorts on a y-axis and the percentage of total population on an x-axis. The term population pyramid is used to refer to such age-sex diagrams because the shape of these diagrams is pyramidal in developing countries, that is, in the peripheral regions of the world-economy. This pyramidal shape indicates a population that is "young" and growing. Birth rates and fertility rates (discussed below) are relatively high, and life expectancies are relatively low. Thus, a substantial proportion of the population in the peripheral countries is very young, under 15 years of age, while the number of people in higher age cohorts, above 60, is very low. By contrast, in the core and parts of the semi-periphery, age-sex diagrams tend to have a rectangular shape. These countries have low birth and fertility rates, and higher life expectancies, and thus, the population is more evenly distributed among age cohorts. These populations are "old" and stable.

Demographic Cycles

If we examine past patterns of population growth rates in different parts of the world, we can identify demographic stages through which populations tend to pass. Where a country is concerning this cycle (that is, what stage the country is in) tends to mirror economic development. We can discern these cycles and stages by examining the relationship between three major indictors: the **crude birth rate**, defined as the number of live births per 1,000 persons per year; the **crude death rate**, defined as the number of deaths per 1,000 persons per year; and the **total fertility rate**, defined as the average number of children born to women of childbearing age (roughly 15–45) during their lifetimes. We can compute the **rate of natural increase** for a given country by subtracting the crude death rate from the crude birth rate. For example, if the crude death birth rate of a country is 20/1,000 and the crude birth rate is 5/1,000, then the natural increase is 15/1,000, or a rate of 1.5% per annum. Death rates do not vary substantially from core to periphery. Indeed, some core countries have higher death rates than some of the poorest countries in the world (see Table 1.1). Only in areas of famine or economic and political unrest (and such occurrences are usually short-lived) are death rates inordinately high. This is largely due to advancements in medical technology, especially immunizations for diseases that used to kill millions of people every year. Such technology has become available in the last 50 years even in some of the poorest countries in the world. On the other hand, as can be seen in Table 1.1, birth rates and fertility rates, and thus rates of natural increase, vary substantially between the core and periphery.

CORE-PERIPHERY POPULATION PATTERNS

As mentioned above, populations tend to pass through stages, and these are revealed by comparing long-term historical patterns for the relationship between birth rates, death rates, and the rate of natural increase. This historical model of population change is usually called the **Demographic Transition Model**, of which there are four stages (Figure 5.1). In Stage 1, birth rates and death rates are both very high, resulting in relatively low or fluctuating rates of natural increase. Until the Industrial Revolution, when societies around the world were still agricultural in nature, all world populations were in Stage 1, but today, there are virtually no populations in this stage. In Stage 2, death rates fall off substantially but birth rates remain

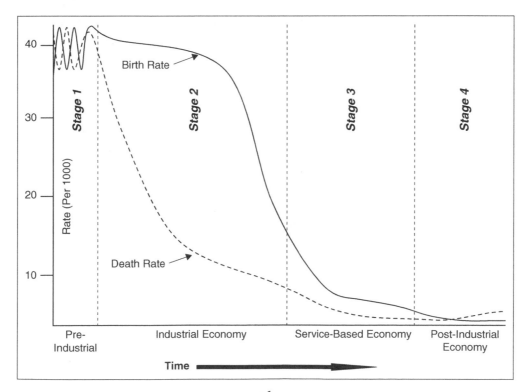

Figure 5.1 The Demographic Transition Model

high, resulting in very high rates of natural increase. In Europe, this stage began around the middle of the eighteenth century, as economies and societies began to industrialize. New medical technology greatly reduced death rates, but birth rates and fertility rates remained very high due to advances in medicine and improved agricultural yields because of more efficient agricultural techniques and tools. With enough food to go around, most people saw little need to alter traditional conceptualizations and norms concerning reproduction. This rapid and exponential growth in population in Stage 2 is the "transition" in populations that the Demographic Transition Model refers to. Today, most countries in the periphery, and some in the semi-periphery, are in Stage 2 of this demographic transition.

In Stage 3 of the Demographic Transition Model, death rates remain quite low and birth and fertility rates begin to drop dramatically, resulting in decreasing rates of natural increase. Most of Europe and North America went through this stage during the late nineteenth and early twentieth centuries as these regions developed mature industrial economies. Today, most of the semi-periphery of the world-economy is in Stage 3. By Stage 4, which began sometime in the late twentieth century in most of the core, birth rates had fallen so much that some countries had approached **zero population growth**. Indeed, in a handful of core countries today (mainly in northern and eastern Europe), populations are actually declining. The populations in the core regions of the world-economy have passed through each of these stages, and today, they are the only regions in Stage 4 of the model.

Why is there such a strong correlation between economic development and fertility, and what factors account for these global patterns? These are extremely complex questions, for which there are few easy answers. We can, however, identify some of the most probable explanations. To be sure, traditional values and customs concerning reproduction and conceptualizations of femininity and masculinity, as well as traditional religious customs, in the folk cultures of the periphery are part of the explanation. Access to modern forms of birth control (expanded in the core, more limited in the periphery) may also help to explain these patterns. But, we could argue that both of these explanations fail to consider the power that women have in most societies around the world about reproductive choice. They also fail to address differences in economies and lifestyles between the core and periphery. The most likely and most plausible explanation for the correlation between fertility and economic development is that the role of women in the societies of the core and periphery are quite different. In the subsistence agricultural societies of the periphery, the role of a woman is often what we might call traditional—they are not only mothers, but also farmers. In such societies, traditional conceptualizations of women and children predominate, and in these traditional economies, children are an economic asset—the more hands for the fields, the better. On the other hand, in the core regions of the world-economy, post-modern ideas have led to radical critiques of such traditional roles for women. In most of the core societies, the role of a woman is not seen as just a mother, but also as a breadwinner. Also in these post-industrial economies where very few people farm for a living and where the costs of living are substantial, children are in fact an economic liability. In the core, then, women have embraced other roles and put off having children until later in life. This change has resulted in drastically lower fertility rates, since waiting to have children until later in life statistically reduces how many children a woman can have.

In summary, population problems in the periphery and parts of the semi-periphery involve those of an ecological nature. These populations are in Stage 2 of the demographic transition, with very high rates of natural increase. But, at the same time, these are precisely the places that are least able to cope with young and growing populations, mostly due to weakly developed political and economic infrastructures. In short, there are increasingly too many people and not enough resources to go around—not only food resources, but other resources such as fuel and clean water. In the core and parts of the semi-periphery, the issues are quite different. These societies are in either Stage 3 or Stage 4 of the demographic transition, with low birth and fertility rates and increasingly older populations. While the advanced post-industrial economies of the core would be able to cope with larger populations, they are precisely the places where rates of natural increase are the lowest. Here, the most pressing issues related to population involve questions of how to cope with an aging population in which more and more older people who are not working must be supported by fewer and fewer people of working age. This is an especially significant problem in core societies having substantial social welfare systems, where governments are in charge of funding retirement and pension plans.

Different societies are approaching such problems in different ways, with varying results. In India, for example, the population is now over 1 billion and is growing quite rapidly, at just under 2% per annum. In the 1970s, India's federal government attempted to take an active role in population reduction by opening family planning clinics, dispersing contraceptives, and appealing to the patriotism of the population through public relations campaigns and advertisements. These efforts, however, have been met with much public resistance because they do not dovetail well with traditional Indian ideas about reproduction and the family. The results of the government's efforts have been mixed at best, and India's population continues to grow rapidly. Another example of governmental intervention in population growth is China. In the early 1980s, the Chinese government, a very powerful one-party system, took an active and rather forceful role in population reduction. Laws were enacted that gave tax breaks and other incentives to couples who chose to have no children. A one-child-only policy was also enacted and rigidly enforced; it limited each couple in the country to only having one child. The government also used public relations campaigns and advertisements to appeal to the patriotism of its citizenry. The results of such policies were quite different from those in India. In 1970, the rate of natural increase was 2.4%, but it had dropped to 1.2% by 1983 and 1.0% in 1997. This success, however, came with some significant social costs. For example, a heavy male gender imbalance now exists in China because of an increase in abortions of female fetuses due to traditional Chinese ideals about inheritance.

POPULATION THEORY

The issue of population has attracted the attention of large numbers of writers and social scientists over the past two centuries. Probably the most famous of these was the English writer **Thomas Malthus**, whose *Essay on the Principle of Population* (1798) set in motion a long-running debate regarding population growth that continues to this day. Malthus was writing at a time when England was in Stage 2 of the demographic transition and was experiencing exponential population growth. Malthus argued that while population was growing exponentially, food supplies were only growing arithmetically, and therefore, they would not be able to keep up with the demand for food. This, he wrote, would at some point result in a crisis punctuated by famine and social collapse.

Obviously, the crisis that Malthus predicted did not come to fruition, for he failed to predict new agricultural technologies and techniques that revolutionized agriculture in the nineteenth and twentieth centuries. These new technologies (such as crop rotation schemes, irrigation technologies, and scientific genetic hybrids) greatly increased the amount of food that could be produced, even in some of the poorest countries in the world. Malthus' failings attracted many critics. Marxist thinkers, for example, argue that the real problem facing the world is not overpopulation, but the fact that the world's resources are not equally shared or distributed and are co-opted by the capitalist class. Another critic, **Esther Boserup**, has argued that population growth does not *necessarily* produce significant problems; it could in fact stimulate economic growth and better food production technology as it did in Europe in previous centuries. But, populations in peripheral countries are increasing at unprecedented rates, and many of these countries have more poor people than ever even though food production has in general increased substantially over the past few decades. These alarming trends have caused some experts to reevaluate Malthus' theory, taking into account not just food, but a variety of other natural resources. These so-called **Neo-Malthusians** argue that Malthus erred in the sense that he wrote only of food and not of other natural resources, but that his overall idea was correct. They contend that population growth in the developing world is a very real and very serious problem because the billions of very poor people that will be added to the world's population in the coming centuries will result in an ever-increasing desperate search for food and natural resources punctuated by more wars, civil strife, pollution, and environmental degradation.

KEY TERMS TO KNOW

Crude Population Density

Physiologic Population
  Density

Doubling Rate

Population Pyramid

Crude Birth Rate

Crude Death Rate

Total Fertility Rate

Rate of Natural Increase

Demographic Transition
  Model

Zero Population Growth

Thomas Malthus

Esther Boserup

Neo-Malthusians

STUDY QUESTIONS

1. Compare and contrast the structure of populations in the core, semi-periphery, and periphery of the world-economy today.

_____

_____

_____

_____

_____

_____

_____

_____

2. What are the main issues concerning population that affect the core regions of the world-economy? What issues affect the peripheral regions?

_____

_____

_____

_____

_____

_____

_____

_____

_____

3. What main factors account for differences in birth rates, fertility rates, and rates of natural increase between the core and the periphery today?

_____

_____

_____

_____

_____

_____

_____

_____

FURTHER READING

Stephen Castles and Mark J. Miller, *The Age of Migration: International Population Movements in the Modern World*, 4th ed. (New York: Guilford Press, 2009).

Paul R. Ehrlich and Anne H. Ehrlich, *The Population Explosion* (New York: Touchstone, 1991).

W.T.S. Gould, *Population and Development* (New York: Routledge, 2009).

Michael R. Haines and Richard H. Steckel, eds., *A Population History of North America* (Cambridge: Cambridge University Press, 2000).

Richard Jackson and Neil Howe, *The Graying of the Great Powers: Demography and Geopolitics in the 21st Century* (Washington: Center for Strategic and International Studies, 2008).

Massimo Livi-Bacci, *A Concise History of World Population*, 4th ed. (New York: Wiley-Blackwell, 2006).

T. R. Malthus, *An Essay on the Principle of Population* (Dover: Dover Publications, 2007).

Laurie Mazur, ed., *A Pivotal Movement: Population, Justice, and the Environmental Challenge* (Washington: Island Press, 2009).

K. Bruce Newbold, *Six Billion Plus: World Population in the Twenty-First Century*, 2nd ed. (New York: Rowman & Littlefield, 2006).

Fred Pearce, *The Coming Population Crash: And Our Planet's Surprising Future* (London: Beacon Press, 2010).

WEB SITES

U.S. Census Bureau (**www.census.gov**)

The World Bank (**www.worldbank.org**)

Population Reference Bureau (**www.prb.org**)

WORLD POLITICAL GEOGRAPHY

In This Chapter:

For most people, the term *political* brings to mind things like elections, political parties, and vigorous partisan debates about various issues that dominate the airwaves and that are so much a part of our current popular culture. While these concepts are each certainly political in nature, in an academic sense, *political* refers largely to the structure and function of governments, issues related to territoriality, and power structures in various types of societies. **Political geography**, then, is the sub-field of human geography that involves the analysis of the spatial expression of these issues. How do people govern themselves, and how has this changed over time? How are governments structured in different parts of the world-economy? What are the spatial characteristics of different types of political organization around the world? This chapter addresses these and other issues.

TYPES OF HISTORICAL POLITICAL ORGANIZATION

In Chapter 1, we outlined the world-systems model of social and political change over time. World-systems analysts argue that, historically, there have been only three types of political, social, and economic organizations: mini-systems, world-empires, and the capitalist world-economy. We can more fully understand such historical change by coupling the world-systems model with descriptions of societal structure borrowed from the fields of anthropology and political geography. Anthropologists and political geographers generally identify five different types of political organization that have occurred throughout human history, four of which can still be observed in societies today:

Band Societies

A **band society** is one in which the there are no formal positions of power and in which members of the society are united by ethnicity, cultural traditions, and kinship. Bands are usually quite small, perhaps only a few dozen extended families, and order is based in and around these extended nuclear families. Such societies exhibit no formal political claim to territory, with the exception, perhaps, of a claimed hunting territory. Strong territorial identity, however, is often associated with cultural identity. Until the Neolithic Revolution, most human societies were organized in such a manner, but few examples survive today. Band societies are limited to a few populations in southwest Africa, parts of tropical Southeast Asia, and some tropical rainforest regions such as the Amazon River basin of South America.

Tribal Societies

A **tribal society** is comprised of a few, perhaps many, bands of people united by common descent, linguistic similarity, and cultural values and traditions. Political leadership in these societies usually is transitory and determined by virtue of perceived courage, bravery, or wisdom. Tribes are largely egalitarian in nature with respect to the communal use of resources and formalized class structures. Tribes usually claim a home *territory*, but the defense of this territory is rarely undertaken with organized military power. Nevertheless, as is the case with band societies, tribal societies exhibit a very strong identity with a specific territory that is often conceived of as a people's *homeland*. Many societies around the world today can be described as tribal in nature. The vast majority of these societies are located in the periphery and in some parts of the semi-periphery of the world-economy: much of sub-Saharan Africa, parts of tropical Southeast Asia, parts of Southwest Asia, and parts of Middle and South America. In world-systems analysis, both band and tribal societies are considered as *mini-systems* in which production and exchange (mode of production) is largely egalitarian and reciprocal in nature. Tribal societies today, however, are also part of the capitalist world-economy, whose economies and societies are increasingly influenced by it.

Chiefdoms

A **chiefdom** describes a feudal social and economic order in which a powerful royal and aristocratic elite in a centralized control center controls the production and redistribution of agricultural products from different parts of a claimed political territory. World-systems analysis refers to this organization as the *redistributive-tributary* mode of production. Leadership in such societies is hereditary (by blood birth), and leaders often claim special divine authority to rule. Chiefdom societies are highly stratified by royalty and occupation, and social rank is largely determined by birth. Agricultural surpluses are generated by coercion of a large peasant class through peonage, serfdom, or slavery. These surpluses are then collected, controlled, stored, and redistributed to the rest of the society by the royalty and aristocracy living in a central urban control center. Chiefdoms usually claim large territories, from which natural resources and agricultural products are extracted, and raise large, organized militaries to defend these territories by force. The central geographical feature of the societies is the *city-state*. World-systems analysis refers to this type of political and social organization as a *world-empire*. Today, there are no surviving examples of chiefdoms. They were at one time, however, found all over the world, emerging after the Neolithic Revolution in the various so-called culture hearths: Mesopotamia, the Nile Valley, lowland Middle America, West and Southeast Africa, northern China, and the Indus Valley. This political and social organization also describes the situation in feudal Europe and Japan.

States

A **state** is an independent political unit occupying a defined, well-populated territory, the borders of which are recognized by surrounding states and militarily defended. All of the countries of the world today are in this sense states.

This type of political organization represents a significant departure from that of bands, tribes, and chiefdoms for territory; cultural or ethnic affiliation is the basis of organization. Most of the world's states are multi-ethnic and multi-cultural in nature, and thus, they are not defined by a certain culture, language, or religion, but rather by place, by a territory. This basis of political organization developed in several areas around the world as feudal orders ended, especially in Europe and East Asia.

All states have a government, within which political institutions of the state function to exert control over the state's population and territory. Through such political power, governments are empowered to impose laws, exact taxes, and wage wars. The structure of this empowerment is basically found in two different forms of internal state political structure today. In **unitary states**, governmental power and authority is centralized in a very strong central government operating from the state's capital city. The vast majority of the nearly 200 states in the world today are unitary states. A handful of states today, however, are **federal states**, in which governmental power and authority is vested in several different levels. There is thus a hierarchy of power from the national level (federal governments) to the regional level (state or provincial governments) to the local level (city governments). Authority and control in states are vested in governments, but for those governments to have *political legitimacy,* they must have some sort of ideology behind it that unites disparate groups within the society. Brute force, through the use of the military for example, may work in the short run, but without some central integrating philosophy behind it (such as freedom or democracy in the United States), a state's government can lose legitimacy and find its right to govern questioned by those it governs.

Nation-States

The idea of the nation-state emerged in Europe in the eighteenth and nineteenth centuries. By definition, a **nation-state** is a state (a territory) that is inhabited by a group of people (a nation) bound together by a general sense of cohesion resulting from a common history, ancestry, language, religion, and political philosophy. A *nation* in this sense refers not to a country, but to a group of people, and a *state* refers to a political territory. The ideal of the nation-state, then, combines these two concepts. As such, this type of political organization involves very strong allegiance to nationality and to territory on the part of the nation-state's citizenry. This political ideal probably first emerged after the Industrial Revolution in Europe as improved communication and transportation technologies enabled more efficient control of large territories. All of the major European colonial powers developed a strong nation-state ideal of political organization in the eighteenth and nineteenth centuries and later exported this ideal all around the world as European power and influence grew very strong during the colonial era.

CORE-PERIPHERY PATTERNS OF POLITICAL COHESIVENESS

Today, all of the countries of the world-economy are politically organized as a *state*, but most aspire to the ideal of the *nation-state*. In practice, however, there are very few true nation-states as the term is defined above: one *nation* of people living in and claiming a defined political territory as its homeland. Why is this? To begin with, even in the strongest nation-states there are always threats to national cohesion. Economic inequality, racial and/or ethnic hostilities and injustices, or perceived disenfranchisement on the part of certain groups in a society may threaten national ideals. But, the biggest obstacle to the ideal of the nation-state is the increasingly globalized world that has emerged since the Merchant Capitalist Revolution. Large-scale migrations (some voluntary, some involuntary) during this era, which continue today, have resulted in the creation of states that are fundamentally multi-national in nature, plural societies in which a variety of ethnic and national groups count themselves as citizens.

Some of the strongest (politically speaking) of such **multi-national states** have developed a strong sense of nationality in spite of the plural nature of the society. In some instances, this occurred by happenstance as a result of a group or groups of people occupying a large territory over a long period (e.g., the European nation-states). In other instances, strong central governments sought to foster nationality overtly through public education systems and the development of a strong sense of patriotism (e.g., the United States, the Soviet Union, and China).

At the other end of the spectrum, multi-national states without a central organizing principal can sometimes degenerate into civil war or ethnic conflict in which various nations of a state struggle for political power (the former Yugoslavia and present-day conflicts in Africa, for example). At the same time, nations of people without their own state often engage in violence to achieve their own state and thus their own political power. Ongoing examples of such conflicts include the struggle of Palestinians, Kurds, and Basques to forge independent governments and states. Most such struggles, civil war, and political instability in general occur today in the periphery and parts of the semi-periphery of the world-economy. While the core states are not without their conflicts, such states usually have very strong central governments that may seek to quell such conflicts. Ethnic problems and conflicts are also usually worked out in the core through democratic processes or through public debate, both of which are relatively peaceful methods compared to the civil wars and military coups that are common in the periphery.

Political cohesiveness in most states today is influenced by two main types of forces working in society. **Centripetal political forces** are those that tend to bring together disparate groups in multi-ethnic, multi-national states. Such forces might include:

- Nationalism—identification with the state and acceptance of its national goals, ideals, and way of life

- Iconography—symbols of unification (flags, national heroes, rituals and holidays, patriotic songs, royalty, etc.)
- Institutions—national education systems, armed forces, state churches, common language
- Effective state organization and administration—public confidence in the organization of the state, security from aggression, fair allocation of resources, equal opportunity to participate, law and order, efficient transportation and communication networks

On the other hand, **centrifugal political forces** are those that tend to destabilize a society and pull disparate groups apart in multi-ethnic and multi-national societies. Examples of centrifugal forces might include:

- Internal discord and challenge to the authority of the state, which can lead to **political devolution** in which national or ethnic groups seek to form separate political authority
- Ethnic separatism and regionalism—this is often seen in states where disparate populations have not been fully integrated (nations without states); this can lead to **Balkanization** in which multi-national states break apart along ethnic lines
- Trouble integrating peripheral locations—this is especially a problem where disparate rural populations are located far away from the capital
- Social and economic inequality—this is most often seen in multi-nation states where the dominant group is seen to exploit minority groups in terms of control of wealth and social services, etc.

KEY TERMS TO KNOW

Political Geography	Unitary State	Centrifugal Political Forces
Band Society	Federal State	Political Devolution
Tribal Society	Nation-State	Balkanization
Chiefdom	Multi-National State	
State	Centripetal Political Forces	

STUDY QUESTIONS

1. Compare and contrast the term *nation* with the term *nation-state*. How are these two types of political organization different?

_____

_____

_____

_____

_____

_____

_____

_____

2. Based on discussions in class and the material in this chapter, can the United States be considered a nation-state? Why or why not?

_____

_____

_____

_____

_____

_____

_____

_____

_____

3. What kinds of political forces are most dominant in the three regions of the world-economy today?

_____

_____

_____

_____

_____

_____

_____

_____

FURTHER READING

John Agnew, *Hegemony: The New Shape of Global Power* (Philadelphia: Temple University Press, 2005).

John Agnew, Katharyne Mitchell, and Gerard Toal, eds., *A Companion to Political Geography* (New York: Wiley-Blackwell, 2007).

John Agnew, *Globalization and Sovereignty* (New York: Rowman & Littlefield, 2009).

Saul B. Cohen, *Geopolitics of the World System*, 2nd ed. (New York: Rowman & Littlefield, 2008).

Kevin Cox, *Political Geography: Territory, State, and Society* (New York: Wiley-Blackwell, 2002).

Jason Dittmer, *Popular Culture, Geopolitics and Identity* (New York: Rowman & Littlefield, 2010).

Wilma Dunaway,

Colin Flint and Peter Taylor, *Political Geography: World-Economy, Nation-State and Locality*, 5th ed. (New York: Prentice-Hall, 2007).

Francis Fukuyama, *State Building: Governance and World Order in the 21st Century* (Ithaca: Cornell University Press, 2004).

Derek Gregory, *The Colonial Present: Afghanistan, Palestine, Iraq* (New York: Wiley-Blackwell, 2004).

Gerry Kearns, *Geopolitics and Empire: The Legacy of Halford Mackinder* (Oxford: Oxford University Press, 2009).

Baldev Raj Nayar, *The Geopolitics of Globalization: The Consequences for Development* (Oxford: Oxford University Press, 2007).

Edward Said, *Orientalism* (New York: Vintage, 1979).

Joanne Sharp, *Geographies of Postcolonialism* (London: Sage Publications, 2008).

THE GEOGRAPHY OF THE WORLD-ECONOMY

In This Chapter:

In previous chapters, we have discussed the structure of the world-economy and defined the core, semi-periphery, and periphery. This chapter examines the nature of economic activities in the three regions of the world-economy in greater detail. How do people make a living in different parts of the world? How has globalization influenced the structure of the world-economy? What factors determine what kind of economic activities are undertaken in certain places? This chapter addresses these primary questions.

THE CLASSIFICATION OF ECONOMIC ACTIVITIES

Economists identify five different types of economic activities, usually referred to as *sectors* of an economy. This classification of the various sectors of an economy will be employed in this chapter to compare and contrast economic activities, modes of production, and social relations of production in the various regions of the capitalist world-economy of today. The **primary sector** of an economy refers to activities related to the extraction of natural resources. This includes fishing, hunting, lumbering, mining, and agriculture. The **secondary sector** describes so-called heavy or blue-collar manufacturing industries that involve the processing of raw materials (usually natural resources) into finished products. These industries include such activities as steel production, automobile assembly, the production of chemicals, food-processing industries, and paper production.

The following three sectors are defined as service industries, those businesses that provide services to individuals and the community at large. The **tertiary sector** refers to financial, business, professional, and clerical services, including retail and wholesale trade. The **quaternary sector** of an economy describes jobs and industries that involve the processing and dissemination of information, as well as administration and control of various enterprises. These jobs are often described by the term *white collar* and consist of professionals working in a variety of industries such as education, government, research, health care, and information management. Finally, the **quinary sector** refers to high-level management and decision making in large organizations and corporations.

FACTORS IN INDUSTRIAL LOCATION

The location of various types of industrial activities is influenced by a variety of geographical factors. These factors are at work not only at the regional scale, but also at the national and global scale. Among these factors are the following:

- The Costs of Production
  - **Geographically fixed costs**—costs relatively unaffected by location of the enterprise (e.g., capital, interest)
  - **Geographically variable costs**—costs that vary spatially (e.g., labor, land, power, transportation)

- Capitalist Ideology and Logic
  - Since the goal of almost all industries is the minimization of costs and the maximization of profit, the location of an industry is most likely to be where the total costs of production are minimized.
- Complexity of the Manufacturing Process
  - The more interdependent a manufacturing process is, the more its costs of production are affected by location (e.g., steel production).
- Type of Raw Materials Involved in the Manufacturing Process
  - Raw materials that are bulky and heavy, perishable, or undergo great weight loss or gain in processing have the greatest effect on siting
  - Examples: pulp, paper and sawmills; fruit and vegetable canning; meat processing; soft drink canning
- Source of Power
  - Important when a source of power is immovable (e.g., the aluminum industry)
- Costs of Labor (Wages)
- The Market for the Product
  - **Market orientation**—placing the last stage of a manufacturing process as close to the market for that product as possible; products that undergo much weight gain during the manufacturing process (e.g., soft drink canning and bottling)
  - **Raw material orientation**—locating the manufacturing plant as close to the raw material that is used as possible; usually applies in industries that use very heavy or bulky raw materials (e.g.. paper production)
- Transportation Costs
  - Water—the least expensive for of transportation for bulky and heavy goods
  - Rail—also relatively inexpensive for bulky and heavy goods but with less flexible routes
  - Trucking—relatively expensive but carries the advantage of very flexible routes
  - Air—the most expensive form of transportation; employed usually for transporting very valuable goods or those that are time-sensitive (e.g., overnight mail service)

ECONOMIES OF THE SEMI-PERIPHERY AND PERIPHERY

The economies of the periphery and parts of the semi-periphery are dominated by primary economic activities. The vast majority of people in the periphery, as illustrated in the socio-economic data in Table 1.1, live in rural areas and make their living from **subsistence farming**. Subsistence farming systems involve agricultural activities that are undertaken not necessarily for money profit, but rather for daily sustenance. Three main types of subsistence agricultural systems are dominant in the peripheral regions of the world-economy today:

Shifting Cultivation

Shifting cultivation, sometimes called *slash-and-burn agriculture*, involves a complex set of farming practices employed in tropical wet regions where environmental conditions (heavy annual rainfall and very poor soils) are delicately balanced. This ancient practice probably dates back to the earliest stages of the Neolithic Revolution and represents a fairly sound ecological solution to the vagaries of life in such an environment. Shifting cultivation cannot support very large populations because tropical soils do not support the kinds of crops that can feed very large populations (such as grain crops). Rather, it involves the use of low-technology tools such as machetes, hoes, digging sticks, and fire to harvest crops such as bananas, taro, cassava, and manioc. Very small groups (bands and tribes) practice a nomadic or semi-nomadic lifestyle and practice shifting cultivation in which a small area is cleared of brush with a machete, covered to allow it to dry, and burned, which fixes nitrogen into the soil. Plants that reproduce vegetatively (like those listed above) are then planted in the ashes. After one or two growing cycles, the soils are exhausted and the group moves on to another site. This lifestyle is practiced mainly in tropical rainforest regions today by a relatively small number of people in locations such as the Amazon and Orinoco basins of South America, parts of Java and other Indonesian islands, parts of tropical central Africa, and parts of Middle America and the Caribbean islands.

Pastoral Nomadism

Pastoral nomadism, sometimes called *extensive subsistence agriculture*, describes the practice of following or hunting herds of game or herding domesticated animals. It is practiced by large numbers of people in tropical grassland environments (savannahs) in central and east-central Africa and some mid-latitude grasslands regions in central Asia. Pastoral nomadism involves an almost wholly nomadic lifestyle that is extensive in its use of land since livestock like cattle, sheep, and goats require much land per animal to thrive. Contrary to popular belief, most pastoral nomads each meat very infrequently because the animals they herd are the main source of wealth and income. Such societies are usually tribal in nature, and the lifestyle involves seasonal movements to greener grazing lands. As such, there are few permanent settlements in the areas where pastoral nomadism is the dominant economic activity.

Intensive Subsistence Farming

Intensive subsistence farming refers to the subsistence production of a variety of grains and vegetables on small, permanent plots that are farmed intensively the year round. This is possible because such farming activities are undertaken mainly in wet regions of the sub-tropics. The most important of these regions and the most important crops are: China, India, and southeast Asia (Vietnam, Thailand, Cambodia, Laos, Myanmar), where rice is the most important crop; Middle America, where beans and corn are dominant; Southwest Asia from Syria to Pakistan, where wheat and rice are most widely grown; and central Africa, where millet, sorghums, and peanuts are very important. This is not to say that these are the only crops grown in these areas. In fact, intensive subsistence agriculture usually involves the production of a large variety of fruits, grains, and vegetables, but at a relatively small scale. Intensive subsistence agricultural systems employ relatively low-technology tools and innovations such as animal-drawn plows, manure for fertilizer, terracing systems, and not a small amount of human muscle power. These farming systems are undertaken by literally millions of people in much of the periphery and semi-periphery. Indeed, rice, the most important grain crop in the world, sustains at least half of the world's population on a daily basis.

Plantation Agriculture

A final important type of agricultural system undertaken primarily in the periphery and semi-periphery of the world-economy today is **plantation agriculture**. While all of the other forms of agriculture in these regions of the world-economy are subsistence in nature, plantation agriculture is a form of **commercial farming** in which the main goal is the maximization of profit per unit area of land under cultivation to sell the products in the international marketplace. Plantation agriculture involves the commercial production of tropical and sub-tropical products, such as tropical fruits, sugar, coffee, tea, and cocoa. A plantation is a large farm on which usually only one crop is grown. Most plantations are owned and managed by large multi-national corporations in the core but employ local low-wage labor. The capital input, as well as the main market for the crops grown on such plantations, is in the core regions of the world-economy. Thus, most plantation products are grown explicitly for export to the core. A British and Dutch innovation, the idea of the plantation dates from the colonial era when British, French, and Dutch companies established sugar plantations using African slave labor in the Caribbean. Plantations were also established in other colonial areas to produce a variety of valuable tropical agricultural crops: tea in India, spices in Indonesia, and coffee in Africa and parts of Middle and South America. Today, most plantations are found in the Caribbean, Central America, and tropical central Africa.

Manufacturing

As discussed in Chapter 1, the globalization of the post-industrial era has created a global economy that is punctuated by an international division of labor in which the periphery and the semi-periphery play an increasingly important role. In the semi-periphery, the post-industrial era ushered in an era in which manufacturing activities have become an important element of most economies. Semi-peripheral economies today are characterized by a mix of subsistence and commercial farming (mostly plantation agriculture) and light and heavy manufacturing activities that employ low-wage, low-skilled urban workers. Most manufacturing enterprises and plantations, however, are owned and managed by multinational corporations in the core—the United States, Japan, and Europe. This pattern has developed over the past 30 years because of evolving service economies in the core and the movement of manufacturing activities out of the core in search of lower costs of production, especially wages. Some of the industries most affected by this transition are textiles (clothing and shoes), inexpensive retail goods (toys, for example), and automobile assembly. Thus, an international division of labor punctuated by multinational companies in the core has evolved into what characterizes it today: high-wage service sector labor in the core; low-wage, low-skilled secondary sector (manufacturing) jobs in the semi-periphery; and low-wage, low-skilled primary sector jobs (subsistence agriculture and plantation enterprises) in the periphery.

ECONOMIES OF THE CORE

Primary Activities

Commercial agricultural activities in the core regions of the world-economy are punctuated by several distinguishing characteristics. First, agriculture employs a very small number of people, but it is nevertheless very productive and remains an important part of core economies. But, agriculture has undergone immense changes in the core over the past 50 years: the number of farmers has drastically declined, the average farm size has grown substantially, and many agricultural activities are increasingly being controlled by large corporations (this is known as **agribusiness**). Farming in the core today is characterized by high inputs of capital, heavy mechanization, the heavy use of hybrid crop and animal varieties, chemical fertilizers, and relatively low inputs of human labor. While such innovations have put many farmers in the core out of work or made them redundant, agricultural production in the core is the highest in the world in terms of crop and animal yields per unit area.

Five main types of farming systems dominate the agricultural economies of the core. First, **commercial dairying** involves the production of milk and milk products, primarily for large urban markets. While fresh milk production is located in the urban hinterlands of most large metropolitan areas in the core (because it is perishable), the production of milk products like cheese, yogurt, and butter is concentrated in the northern United States and northern and Alpine Europe. Second, **market gardening**, sometimes called "truck farming," involves the commercial production of fruits, vegetables, or other specialized crops, again mainly for large urban markets. Market gardening is concentrated along the Atlantic coast of the United States from New Jersey to Florida to Texas, parts of coastal California, northwestern Europe (especially the Netherlands), parts of coastal Japan, and parts of Australia and New Zealand. Third, **mixed livestock and grain farming** refers to the production of livestock for human consumption alongside the production of grains (mainly corn and wheat) for use as livestock fodder. This describes the agricultural systems dominant in the Great Plains (wheat and cattle) and Midwest (corn, soybeans, hogs, and cattle) of the United States, the Pampas of Argentina (wheat, corn, and cattle), much of central Europe (sorghum, corn, cattle, and hogs), and the interior grasslands of Australia (wheat and sheep). Fourth, **livestock ranching** involves the commercial production of livestock (mainly cattle) for large urban markets and for international export. Ranching takes place mainly in semi-arid grassland environments of the mid-latitude regions of the core: the interior West of the United States, interior Australia, southern Brazil, parts of Argentina, and parts of Spain and Greece. Finally, **Mediterranean agriculture** involves the production of highly specialized Mediterranean crops like grapes, figs, dates, olives, and citrus fruits. Such activities are undertaken in regions around the world with the distinctive Mediterranean climate (hot, dry summers and cool, wet winters): southern California, the circum-Mediterranean, southwest Australia, parts of southwestern Africa, and parts of Chile.

Service Activities

The economies of the core regions of the capitalist world-economy were built upon a factory organization of labor and a reliance on heavy manufacturing industrial activity during the nineteenth and early twentieth centuries. But, the last 30 years have witnessed a vast shift in how core economies are structured. In search of lower costs of labor, many large corporations have spearheaded the development of an international division of labor in which manufacturing activities (and manufacturing jobs along with them) have been moved to semi-peripheral locations. Today, the vast majority of the population in core regions is employed in the service sector of the economy, especially the tertiary and quaternary sectors. Core economies are also increasingly information-based: some of the largest companies in the world, like AT&T and Microsoft, are in the business of perfecting and selling the access and dissemination of information.

This business has resulted in revolutionary changes in the industrial landscape of the core countries and the geography of industry and manufacturing in these places. The once-dominant industrial centers such as the Great Lakes region in the United States, the British Midlands, and the German Ruhr district have now become "rust belts." Entirely new manufacturing centers have now developed in places in which the main resource for new information technologies, human brainpower, is nearby. Examples of these new manufacturing regions include Silicon Valley in northern California, the Research Triangle of North Carolina, and the "Golden Triangle" of central Texas. In Europe, such centers have been developed in many areas of eastern Europe, such as eastern Germany, the Czech Republic, Hungary, and Poland.

KEY TERMS TO KNOW

Primary Sector

Secondary Sector

Tertiary Sector

Quaternary Sector

Quinary Sector

Geographically Fixed
  Costs

Geographically Variable
  Costs

Market Orientation

Raw Material Orientation

Subsistence Farming

Commercial Farming

Shifting Cultivation

Pastoral Nomadism

Intensive Subsistence
  Farming

Plantation Agriculture

Agribusiness

Commercial Dairying

Market Gardening

Mixed Livestock and Grain
  Agriculture

Livestock Ranching

Mediterranean
  Agriculture

STUDY QUESTIONS

1. Compare and contrast agricultural systems in the periphery, semi-periphery, and periphery.

_____

_____

_____

_____

_____

_____

_____

_____

2. Compare and contrast the defining characteristics of the economies of the core, semi-periphery, and periphery today.

_____

_____

_____

_____

_____

_____

_____

_____

_____

FURTHER READING

Jason Clay, *World Agriculture and the Environment: A Commodity-by-Commodity Guide to Impacts and Practices* (Washington: Island Press, 2004).

Paul K. Conkin, *A Revolution Down on the Farm: The Transformation of American Agriculture Since 1929* (Lexington: The University Press of Kentucky, 2009).

Thomas L. Friedman, *The Lexus and the Olive Tree: Understanding Globalization* (New York: Anchor, 2000).

Anthony Giddens, *Runaway World: How Globalization is Reshaping our Lives* (New York: Routledge, 2002).

David Grigg, *An Introduction to Agricultural Geography* (New York: Routledge, 1995).

David Harvey, *The Limits to Capital* (London: Verso, 2006).

Paul Knox and John Agnew, *The Geography of the World-Economy*, 3rd ed. (New York: John Wiley & Sons, 1998).

Joel Kotkin, *The New Geography: How the Digital Revolution is Reshaping the American Landscape* (New York: Random House, 2001).

Marcel Mazoyer and Laurence Roudart, *A History of World Agriculture: From the Neolithic Age to the Current Crisis* (New York: Monthly Review Press, 2006).

Jan Nederveen Pieterse, *Globalization and Culture: Global Mélange* (New York: Roman & Littlefield, 2009).

Stephen Nottingham, *Eat Your Genes: How Genetically Modified Food is Entering Our Diet* (London: Zed Books, 2003).

Michael Pollan, *The Omnivore's Dilemma: A Natural History of Four Meals* (New York: Penguin, 2007).

Pietra Rivoli, *The Travels of a T-Shirt in the Global Economy* (New York: John Wiley & Sons, 2005).

Robert K. Schaeffer, *Understanding Globalization: The Social Consequences of Political, Economic, and Environmental Change* (New York: Rowman & Littlefield, 2009).

Eric Schlosser, *Fast Food Nation: The Dark Side of the All-American Meal* (New York: Harper, 2009).

Jan Aart Scholte, *Globalization: A Critical Introduction*, 2nd ed. (New York: Palgrave Macmillan, 2005).

Jennifer Thompson, *Genes for Africa: Genetically Modified Crops in the Developing World* (Cape Town: Juta Academic, 2004).

B. L. Turner and Stephen Brush, eds., *Comparative Farming Systems* (New York: Guilford Press, 1987).

World Bank, *World Development Report 2008: Agriculture and Development* (New York: World Bank Publications, 2008).

CHAPTER 8

URBAN LANDSCAPES OF THE WORLD-ECONOMY

In This Chapter:

The previous chapters have outlined the basic structure of the world-economy, especially with respect to relative levels of development and underdevelopment in the core, semi-periphery, and periphery. This final chapter discusses global patterns of urbanization, especially during the post-industrial era of the late twentieth and early twenty-first centuries, within this world-systems context. Although urbanization has been a phenomenon associated with many cultures for thousands of years (since the Neolithic Revolution), the highest rates of urban growth have materialized during the most recent industrial and post-industrial eras. As a result, more people are now living in cities than ever before in human history. Where are the most urbanized places in the world? Where are urban populations growing the fastest? What are the potential consequences of high rates of urban growth in different regions of the world-economy? What are some of the distinguishing characteristics of cities and urban landscapes in the post-industrial era? How do urban landscapes differ in the various regions of the world-economy? This chapter addresses these and other questions.

GLOBAL PATTERNS OF URBANIZATION

A logical place to begin this discussion is with an overview of some general global patterns of urbanization. The most urbanized populations today are in core and semi-peripheral regions. Indeed, of the regions of the world in which 70 percent or more of the population lives in urban areas, all are either in the core or semi-periphery of the world-economy:

- North America (The United States and Canada)
- Mexico
- Northern and Western Europe
- South America (with the exception of the Andean highlands)
- Australia and New Zealand
- Japan and South Korea
- Parts of Southwest Asia and North Africa (Libya, Saudi Arabia, Israel, Jordan, United Arab Emirates)

At the same time, however, data compiled over the last 10 years indicate that urban populations are growing the fastest in the periphery and parts of the semi-periphery. The overall global trend in the post-industrial era, then, has been stagnant or negative rates of urban growth in the core but very high rates of urban growth in the semi-periphery and periphery. The growth of urban populations in the semi-periphery and periphery is cause for concern because these economies can ill afford the social and economic pressures resulting from ever-increasing urban populations. Such pressures might include:

- Housing—to shelter newly arrived migrants (most such migrants in the semi-periphery and periphery have moved from rural areas to urban areas in search of jobs)

- Food—urban dwellers do not produce food, but rather consume food produced in rural areas by fewer and fewer farmers
- Natural resources—clean air and water
- Public services—water and sewage services, trash collection, communication and transportation infrastructures, security (police), social services
- Social problems—crime, ethnic conflict, economic inequalities, unemployment
- Jobs—to provide a living for newly arrived migrants from the rural countryside

For an urban region to function smoothly, each of these factors must be addressed or provided. While similar problems plague all cities worldwide, including those in core regions, core economies are much better equipped to handle large urban populations. In many parts of the periphery and in parts of the semi-periphery, such services are woefully inadequate at best and nonexistent at worst. Large and growing urban populations, then, present such areas with myriad issues and problems, and only add to the many economic and social problems that afflict these areas of the world-economy.

The growth of large cities in the semi-periphery and periphery of the world-economy during the late industrial and early post-industrial eras is illustrated in the following list of the world's largest metropolitan areas in 2014, according to the United Nations:

1. Tokyo, Japan (37.8 million) [*core*]

2. Delhi, India (25 million) [*periphery*]

3. Shanghai, China (23 million) [*semi-periphery*]

4. Mexico City, Mexico (20.8 million) [*semi-periphery*]

5. Sao Paulo, Brazil (20.8 million) [*semi-periphery*]

6. Mumbai, India (20.7 million) [*periphery*]

7. Osaka, Japan (20.1 million) [*core*]

8. Beijing, China (19.5 million) [*semi-periphery*]

9. New York, USA (18.6 million) [*core*]

10. Cairo, Egypt (18.4 million) [*periphery*]

11. Los Angeles, USA (11.8 million) [*core*]

12. Buenos Aires, Argentina (11.2 million) [*semi-periphery*]

13. Rio de Janeiro, Brazil (10.8 million) [*semi-periphery*]

14. Moscow, Russia (10.5 million) [*semi-periphery*]

15. Shanghai, China (10.0 million) [*semi-periphery*]

16. Karachi, Pakistan (9.8 million) [*periphery*]

17. Paris, France (9.6 million) [*core*]

As late as the mid-twentieth century, nearly all of the most populous cities in the world were located in Europe or North America. Today, however, of the 20 largest cities in the world, only six are located in core regions of the world-economy. Eight are in semi-peripheral locations, and six are in the periphery. Thus, while large cities are associated with the wealthiest countries in most people's minds, it is clear that large urban populations are increasingly phenomena of the semi-periphery and periphery as well. Indeed, experts speculate that Mexico City will overtake Tokyo as the world's largest metropolitan area by 2025 and that only two or three cities in core regions (Tokyo-Yokohama, New York, and perhaps Osaka) will remain on the list of the 20 largest cities in the world.

THE NATURE OF CITIES

Why do cities exist in the first place? What advantages are offered by the agglomeration of large populations in a certain place? What functions do cities perform? The answers to these questions are extremely complex and may differ from place to place, not only within the same country, but within the different regions of the world-economy as well. But, we can begin to understand the nature of cities by pointing out a few basic caveats concerning urban regions about which most experts agree:

1. Cities perform certain basic economic functions.
   This is the reason that cities exist at all: for the efficient performance of functions that a population could not perform adequately or efficiently if it were randomly dispersed through space. For example, producers are nearer to the consumers of their products, and workers are nearer to their places of employment. Time, money, and efficiency are saved by the agglomeration of people in space.

2. Cities function as markets.
   This has been the case since the earliest Neolithic Revolutions. As such, they have close reciprocal relationships with their rural hinterlands. For example, cities consume food that is produced primarily in rural areas. Cities are also the places where raw materials from rural areas (such as agricultural products or natural resources) are processed into consumable

goods. Cities dispense goods and services not only for their own urban populations, but for rural populations as well.

3. Cities tend to be located strategically.
Cities are most commonly located at certain advantageous sites:
   - Sites that offer security and/or defense, such as a hilltop or island (many Neolithic and Medieval cities occupy such sites)
   - Sites that are economically advantageous, such as a **head of navigation site** on a river, a river fording or portage site, or a railhead site

4. Cities function as central places.
The idea of cities as "central places" stems from the work of the German geographer Walter Christaller, who in 1933 published a theoretical study concerning the distribution of service centers. Christaller wanted to understand the theoretical spatial patterns that would result when rural residents traded with a central market town providing goods and services. Human geographers call the results of this study **Central Place Theory**. The theory has been applied in many different places around the world to more fully understand urban patterns and appears to have stood the test of time in terms of its explanatory value. Christaller was concerned with why cities are located where they are, why some cities grow while others do not, and why there is an apparently non-random pattern concerning the location of cities relative to other cities. Central Place Theory holds that the importance of a market city is directly related to its centrality—the relative importance of a place with respect to its surrounding region.

The central concept of Central Place Theory concerns the *range* of a good or service—the distance that people are willing to travel to obtain a certain good or service. Some goods and services, such as bread or food in general, are **low-range goods**, those for which people are not willing to travel far to obtain. Others, such as cars or furniture, are **high-range goods**, for which people are willing to travel long distances to buy. Christaller argued that the *centrality,* or relative importance, of a market town or city is directly proportional to the types of goods and services offered there, and that a natural hierarchy of size will arise with respect to market locations based upon what types of goods or services are offered there. This central place hierarchy ranges from **low-order places** that offer only low-range goods, to **high-order places** that offer both low- and high-range goods and services. Central Place Theory thus gives us insight into the functions that cities perform, why some cities grow and others do not, and why there are many small central places but only a few very large central places.

URBAN LANDSCAPES OF THE CORE

The following sections list the distinguishing characteristics of urban regions in selected locations in the core, semi-periphery, and periphery of the world-economy:

The core regions of the world-economy contain some of the largest cities in the world. Several of these cities developed into the nodes or "command and control centers" of the world-economy and remain so today. These so-called **world cities** are distinguished by the following characteristics:

- Financial centers—head offices, stock market locations
- Command and control centers of world capitalist economy—corporate headquarters of multi-national firms
- Political centers
- Cultural centers
- Nodes of international linkages

Western European Cities

Medieval Origins

One of the most striking features of most western European cities today is the juxtaposition of pre-industrial and post-industrial features in the region's urban landscapes. Many western European urban centers can trace their origins to the medieval era (from the tenth to the fifteenth century), when they emerged as high-order places in the central place hierarchy due to economic and/or political importance. The siting and the pre-industrial landscapes of many western European cities reflect these medieval origins, as well as their early roles as transportation centers and economic and political centers. Many of the largest western European cities, for example, are located either on the coast or on a large, navigable river. Some occupy early head-of-navigation sites (London, for example) or river crossing sites (Frankfurt, Germany). Others occupy defensive sites, such as hill-top or island locations, and are often associated with the sites of medieval-era castles and fortifications (Edinburgh, Scotland and Heidelberg, Germany, for example). Another medieval feature of many western European urban landscapes is the seemingly haphazard arrangement of streets, reflective of a lack of centralized city planning and growth by accretion over long periods. Only since the nineteenth and twentieth centuries have many western European cities begun to enact city-planning schemes to alter ancient medieval urban city plans. The presence of straight, ceremonial boulevards, such as the Champs Elysées in Paris and Unter den Linden in Berlin, reflect this kind of centralized city planning.

Abundant "Green" Spaces

Also reflective of the more modern trend toward centralized urban planning is the presence of relatively large areas set aside for public use. Such spaces include pedestrian zones, public markets, and parks. Many western European cities are surrounded by large tracts of forests and parks located at the urban-rural fringe on the outskirts of urban areas; these tracts are collectively known as **greenbelts**.

Dense Public Transportation Networks

Modern western European cities are characterized by well-developed, efficient urban transportation networks. These networks usually include bus, tram (streetcar), subway, and light rail transportation.

"Low" Profiles

Compared to many North American cities, most large western European cities have relatively few tall skyscrapers. With the exception of London, Paris, and Frankfurt, all of which have downtown central business districts with prominent skyscrapers, most European cities have a comparatively low landscape profile comprising many square miles of multi-unit housing structures and retail services.

Emerging Post-Industrial Multiethnic Cities

Although most western European states emerged from the colonial era as very strong nation-states with ethnically homogeneous societies, the late twentieth and early twenty-first centuries have been characterized by significant influxes of ethnic minorities, primarily from southern and eastern Europe, Asia, and Africa. From Moroccans and Algerians in Spain and France, to Indians and Pakistanis in England, to Serbs and Africans in Germany and the Scandinavian countries, the larger urban centers of western Europe have received the largest number of these immigrants; their presence has fundamentally altered the ethnic makeup of the region such that most western European societies can now be characterized as fundamentally multiethnic. Increased immigration has altered European societies in many positive ways, but it has also not occurred without some significant social issues. For example, many of these new immigrants are refugees escaping political and economic turmoil in their home countries, and they arrive in European cities without jobs or housing. Given the immigrants' need for jobs and housing, some cities have experienced significant strains in dealing with large influxes of unemployed immigrants. In response, many cities have constructed several immigrant housing developments in specific areas set aside for such housing, often on the outskirts of urban regions. This practice has created **ethnic enclaves**, neighborhoods that are numerically dominated by specific ethnic groups, with businesses, such as restaurants and retain shops, catering to those groups.

North American Cities

Changing Forms of Transportation

Historically, the most significant factor that has influenced the structure and size of North American cities has been changing dominant forms of transportation over time. In the pre-industrial era—from the colonial period until the late nineteenth century—most cities were oriented toward pedestrian and/or animal transportation. These pedestrian cities tended to be rather compact, with zones of varying land use forming concentric circles around a **central business district** nucleus dominated by retail services and high-rent residential housing. During the early industrial period, between roughly 1880 and 1940, urban transportation came to be dominated by streetcars, subways, and railways. As a result, cities expanded dramatically in size as commuters could now live further from the central business district due to faster and more efficient forms of public transportation. Zones of varying urban land use expanded outward from the central business district along these public transportation arteries. These "streetcar cities" came to resemble a wheel, with the central business district as the hub and railway and streetcar lines as the spokes radiating outward from the center.

After World War II, the widespread use of the automobile as the dominant mode of transportation engendered even more radical changes in the size and shape of American cities. With the construction of interstate highway systems, commuters began to live further and further away from the central city, leading to the development of intense **suburbanization** at the urban-rural fringe dominated by upper-income residential housing and services catering to that income group. Cities expanded dramatically in size such that most American urban regions can now be characterized as comprising multiple "cities within cities," covering hundreds of square miles and connected via a dense and efficient network of large highways.

Spatial Differentiation Based on Ethnicity, Race and Income

One of the most distinctive characteristics of North American cities today is the development of conspicuous sectors of varying residential land use that reflect societal differences in ethnicity, race, class, and income. This has led to the development of distinctive ethnic and class-based neighborhoods within American urban regions. This trend began in the nineteenth and early twentieth centuries with the immigration of millions of Europeans, especially those coming from southern and eastern Europe who settled in the large industrial cities of the Northeast, and the migration of hundreds of thousands of African-Americans from rural areas of the South to industrial cities of the North. Many of these immigrants and migrants settled among one another in distinctive ethnic neighborhoods near central business districts, downtown areas that were abandoned by upper-income whites in favor of suburban locales at the urban-rural fringe.

Zoning

Zoning refers to the detailed urban land-use planning that city governments in the United States undertake; it is yet another distinguishing characteristic of American cities. Through the use and enforcement of zoning laws, city governments have the power to authorize and enforce what types of economic activities can take place in certain areas and what kind of structures can and cannot be built in certain areas. Such areas are said to be "zoned" for certain activities or kinds of structures. Such zoning laws have had a significant impact on the spatial differentiation of American cities with respect to both residential and business land use.

Gentrification

Gentrification refers to the revitalization of formerly abandoned properties in the central business district of American cities, a trend that is increasingly characteristic of American cities in the post-industrial era of the late twentieth and early twenty-first centuries. As upper-income whites moved to suburban areas from the central city during the 1950s, 1960s, and 1970s, and as warehousing and light industry activities also moved to urban peripheral regions during the same period, downtown areas in many American cities fell into disrepair. To revitalize downtown areas and to entice suburbanites back to the central business district, city governments began to support the efforts of wealthy investors in purchasing and revitalizing formerly abandoned downtown properties. These gentrification schemes often involve the construction of pedestrian malls dominated by expensive restaurants and specialty shops that cater to upper-income customers. While these activities have given many downtown areas a second life and contributed to economic revitalization, gentrification does not occur without some social costs. For example, as downtown areas were abandoned during the era of rapid suburban growth, they were often repopulated by lower-income residents and recent immigrants. Because such residents lack the political and economic power of wealthy investors and developers, gentrification schemes often result in such residents being forced to move.

URBAN LANDSCAPES OF THE SEMI-PERIPHERY AND PERIPHERY

Latin American Cities

An Iberian Colonial Imprint

The most conspicuous urban landscape features of Latin American cities reflect the Iberian (Spanish and Portuguese) colonial imprint that is common throughout the region, from the southwestern United States in the north to the southern tip of South America. Spanish colonial goals were focused on the expansion of empire, the expansion of Christendom, and the extraction of valuable natural resources such as gold and silver, and distinctive urban landscape features reflect these colonial goals. For example, to accomplish these goals, the Spanish instituted a centrally planned and ordered network of urban centers that was built upon pre-existing networks of Native American towns. By law and in practice, all Spanish colonial towns were constructed on a rectilinear grid of streets oriented to the cardinal directions surrounding an open, public *plaza*. Almost all colonial towns were associated with *presidios*, forts of garrisoned military troops that exerted political and military control, and cathedrals staffed by Jesuit priests who were charged with converting Native Americans to Christianity. Other Iberian landscape features common in Latin American cities include Spanish architectural features, such as *adobe* construction and red tile roofs.

Spatial Differentiation Reflecting Strong Class Differences

Like other semiperipheral areas of the world-economy, Latin America is a region characterized by relatively intense social stratification based upon class, race, ethnicity, and income. The urban landscapes of the region reflect this stratification. In contrast to American cities, the wealthiest members of Latin American societies often live very near city centers, in elite sectors or neighborhoods. These elite sectors are surrounded by distinctive neighborhood sectors according to race, ethnicity, and income. The poorest members of Latin American societies, especially those that are homeless, live in so-called **squatter belts** in urban-rural fringe areas on the outskirts of cities in very poor conditions devoid of urban services such as running water, electricity, and sewage and trash disposal.

Southeast and South Asian Cities

A Western European Colonial Imprint

In contrast to Iberian colonial goals, the goals of western European colonial powers (such as Holland, England, and France) in South Asia (e.g., Pakistan, India, and Sri Lanka) and Southeast Asia (e.g., Vietnam, Myanmar, and Malaysia) were decidedly merchant capitalist in nature. That is, profit based on the establishment of privately financed plantations specializing in the production of tropical and subtropical agricultural products (such as tea, coffee, sugar, rubber, and spices) was more important than the expansion of the empire. After politically securing a colonial area, private companies typically established plantations in interior areas and warehousing and port facilities on the coast, often at the mouth of a major river. These port cities, which existed prior to European colonialism, came to be remade into European colonial outposts with distinctive European urban landscape features. Such features included European architectural styles employed in the construction of public buildings and the dwellings of European plantation managers, retail services catering to a European clientele, and European schools and churches.

Residential Segregation Based on Income and Class

As is the case in most urban centers around the world, South Asian and Southeast Asian urban residential sectors reflect differences in income and class. Colonial port cities (such as Mumbai and Calcutta in India and Hanoi in Vietnam) are usually characterized by three distinct types of residential zones: 1) an elite, European sector surrounding old warehousing facilities near port zones where European colonial managers and civil servants lived, worked, shopped and sent their children to school; 2) a sector of low-income housing also near historical port and warehousing zones numerically dominated by lower and middle-class workers; and 3) a sector on the outskirts of cities dominated by low-income landless families. These sectors, called **shantytowns**, resemble the squatter belts that can be found on the outskirts of many Latin American cities, and like squatter belts, they lack basic services such as running water, public sewage systems, and electricity.

KEY TERMS TO KNOW

Head of Navigation Site	High-Order Places	Suburbanization
Central Place Theory	World Cities	Zoning
Low-Range Goods	Greenbelts	Gentrification
High-Range Goods	Ethnic Enclaves	Squatter Belts
Low-Order Places	Central Business District	Shantytowns

NAME _____   DATE _____

STUDY QUESTIONS

1. Where are urban populations growing most rapidly in the world today? What are some of the challenges these areas face because of high rates of urban growth?

_____

_____

_____

_____

_____

_____

2. Compare and contrast urban landscapes in the core with those in the semi-periphery and periphery of the world-economy. What characteristics distinguish urban landscapes in each region?

_____

_____

_____

_____

_____

_____

_____

FURTHER READING

Mark Abrahamson, *Global Cities* (Oxford: Oxford University Press, 2004).

Robert Bruegmann, *Sprawl: A Compact History* (Chicago: University of Chicago Press, 2006).

Stanley Brunn, Maureen Hays-Mitchell, and Donald Zeigler, eds., *Cities of the World: World Regional Urban Development*, 4th ed. (New York: Rowman & Littlefield, 2008).

Joel Garreau, *Edge City: Life on the New Frontier* (New York: Anchor, 1992).

Alan Gilbert, *The Mega-City in Latin America* (New York: United Nations University Press, 1996).

Susan Hanson and Genevieve Giuliano, eds., *The Geography of Urban Transportation*, 3rd ed. (New York: Guilford Press, 2004).

R.J. Johnston, *City and Society: An Outline for Urban Geography* (New York: Routledge, 2007).

Yeong-Hyun Kim and John Rennie Short, *Cities and Economies* (New York: Routledge, 2008).

Paul Knox and Steven Pinch, *Urban Social Geography: An Introduction*, 6th ed. (New York: Prentice-Hall, 2009).

Joel Kotkin, *The City: A Global History* (New York: Modern Library, 2006).

James Howard Kunstler, *The Geography of Nowhere: The Rise and Decline of America's Man-Made Landscape* (Washington: Free Press, 1994).

Robert Neuwirth, *Shadow Cities: A Billion Squatters, a New Urban World* (New York: Routledge, 2006).

Lewis Mumford, *The City in History: Its Origins, Its Transformations, and Its Prospects* (New York: Mariner Books, 1968).

David Smith, *Third World Cities in Global Perspective: The Political Economy of Uneven Urbanization* (Boulder: Westview Press, 1996).

INDEX

CPSIA information can be obtained at www.ICGtesting.com
Printed in the USA
LVOW01s0658160515

438549LV00002B/3/P